PRAISE FOR LIFE ON EARTH

"*In* Life on Earth, *masterful teacher and life guide Mike Dooley dives deep into the root of all existence, taking the reader on a fantastic journey of self-discovery and enlightenment. He asks the deep, timeless questions that we all ask ourselves every day, and then provides the profound answers that awaken us to dream, to trust, to thrive, and to lean into our magnificence, which—as he lovingly explains—has been our birthright since time began. He brilliantly navigates the real-world challenges and stumbling blocks of life and inspires us to adventure with him into new realms of understanding. In the process, we are healed, we move beyond our constrictions, and we discover our wholeness.* Life on Earth *is a classic . . . a timeless manifesto of awakening, and a must-read if you're looking to take your life to the next level.*"

— davidji, author of *Secrets of Meditation*

"*A fascinating read. I highly recommend it.*"

— Caroline Myss, author of *Defy Gravity* and *Anatomy of the Spirit*

"*You're holding a literary version of the red pill from* The Matrix. *Open it and see how wild and wonderful the rabbit hole called* Life on Earth *truly is.*"

— Christopher Parker, screenwriter, *Heaven Is for Real*

LIFE

ON

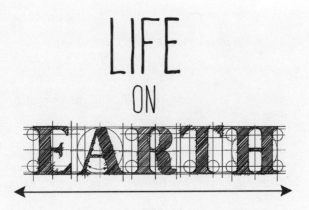

ALSO BY MIKE DOOLEY

BOOKS

The Top 10 Things Dead People Want to Tell YOU*

Leveraging the Universe: 7 Steps to Engaging Life's Magic

Manifesting Change: It Couldn't Be Easier

Infinite Possibilities: The Art of Living Your Dreams

Choose Them Wisely: Thoughts Become Things!

Notes from the Universe: New Perspectives from an Old Friend

More Notes from the Universe: Life, Dreams and Happiness

Even More Notes from the Universe: Dancing Life's Dance

*An Adventurer's Guide to the Jungles of Time and Space
(formerly titled Lost in Space)*

Totally Unique Thoughts: Reminders of Life's Everyday Magic

DVDs

The Path Less Traveled: Performing Miracles

Manifesting Change: It Couldn't Be Easier

Thoughts Become Things

VIDEO COURSES

*Playing the Matrix and Getting What You Really Want**

*A Trainer's Guide to Infinite Possibilities**

FOR CHILDREN

Your Magical Life

Dreams Come True: All They Need Is You

*Available from Hay House
Please visit:

Hay House USA: www.hayhouse.com®
Hay House Australia: www.hayhouse.com.au
Hay House UK: www.hayhouse.co.uk
Hay House South Africa: www.hayhouse.co.za
Hay House India: www.hayhouse.co.in

***

LIFE
ON
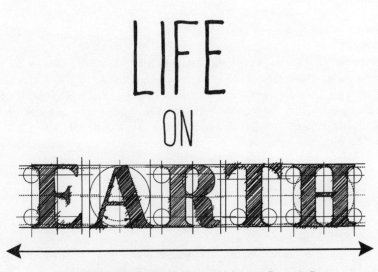
UNDERSTANDING WHO WE ARE,
HOW WE GOT HERE,
AND
WHAT MAY LIE AHEAD

MIKE DOOLEY

HAY HOUSE, INC.
Carlsbad, California • New York City
London • Sydney • Johannesburg
Vancouver • New Delhi

Published and distributed in the United States by: Hay House, Inc.: www.hayhouse
.com® • *Published and distributed in Australia by:* Hay House Australia Pty. Ltd.: www
.hayhouse.com.au • *Published and distributed in the United Kingdom by:* Hay House
UK, Ltd.: www.hayhouse.co.uk • *Published and distributed in the Republic of South
Africa by:* Hay House SA (Pty), Ltd.: www.hayhouse.co.za • *Distributed in Canada by:*
Raincoast Books: www.raincoast.com • *Published in India by:* Hay House Publishers
India: www.hayhouse.co.in

Cover design: Charles McStravick • *Interior design:* Riann Bender

Library of Congress Cataloging-in-Publication Data

Names: Dooley, Mike, 1961- author.
Title: Life on Earth : understanding who you are, why you're here, and what
   may lie ahead / Mike Dooley.
Description: Carlsbad, California : Hay House, Inc., [2016]
Identifiers: LCCN 2016028081 | ISBN 9781401945572 (hardcover : alk. paper)
Subjects: LCSH: Life--Miscellanea. | Wisdom--Miscellanea. |
   Consciousness--Miscellanea.
Classification: LCC BF1999 .D6154 2016 | DDC 158--dc23 LC record available at
https://lccn.loc.gov/2016028081

Hardcover ISBN: 978-1-4019-4557-2

10 9 8 7 6 5 4 3 2 1
1st edition, December 2016

Printed in the United States of America

EVERYONE HAS TIME FOR THIS. THE UPSIDE
IS INSANE—DOMINION OVER ALL THINGS.

←——————————————————————————→

CONTENTS

I have to ask, are there aliens among us?

Is there really a devil in hell? Is there even a hell?

What right do I have to be happy when others are not?

How do we know and find our purpose?

How do we live in the "now" without giving up on our dreams?

INTRODUCTION

Does anyone really know what they want?

Does déjà vu come from knowing someone in a past life?

How can I be happy? Happier? The happiest?

Why does it so often seem that "nice guys finish last"?

What if when we die, that's it?

There are over 4,000 religions; how is anyone supposed to know what the truth is?

If there's a God, why do really awful things happen in this world?

I've lived my life through questions. Asking about almost everything—aliens, UFOs, yetis, ghosts, the pyramids, time travel, God, hypnosis, and mind-power—but mostly questions like *What the hell are we doing here? And then everyone dies? Gone forever? Why bother? What's the point? To be tested, judged, and sentenced?*

And my questions . . . get answered. Wisely. *Really* wisely. Used to scare me. In the beginning, I didn't know how they were answered, when, or by whom. Years later, well into the phenomenon, it dawned on me to ask that question too. And, yeah, I was answered. More on that in a bit.

To this day, my "knowingness" usually arrives invisibly, unannounced, somewhere in the span of weeks or months after I first pose the question; when necessary, I can expect and get an answer while I wait, same day.

Some folks see dead people, others go out-of-body, and I . . . I get answers. Admittedly this "gift" might not sound as impressive as meeting Beethoven, hypothetically, or soaring through time and space like Jonathan Livingston Seagull, but at my age, already having had the chance to ask pretty much *all* of my most profound and piercing questions, I can tell you, it's damn cool. I'd even choose it over meeting Beethoven *and* time travel.

For example, I ask, "What the hell are we here for?"

And I get the answer:

> *You are eternal, spiritual beings, on earth by choice, at an early ebb in the spiritual evolution of your kind. You each chose to be exactly who you now are, possessing the dreams you now have and the challenges you presently face, for the reasons of learning and joy. Among the things you wanted to understand: love is a given, not an option; your thoughts hold the key to living the life of your wildest dreams; and no matter how things appear, your eternal salvation is ensured.*

See? You should try it. Some call it automatic writing, except for me it's not so automatic. And I rarely write any of it down, unless it's in my journal, in which case I usually sit long hours after scribbling a question, staring at blank pages, waiting for a reply. But when it arrives, *shiver-me-timbers*, suddenly where there was once confusion, there's clarity, and sometimes, it's so good I laugh out loud.

> *As you awaken to the truths summoned by your questions and the reasons you chose this lifetime, you'll move on to new and presently unimaginable heights of peace, fulfillment, and joy. You are ultimately destined to discover your power and accept its responsibilities, but how and when you achieve these, in this incarnation or the future, is what makes each lifetime the greatest adventure of all. Similarly, the deciding factor in whether or not you and your civilization will succeed this time is the rate at which you choose to open your hearts and minds to embrace your spiritual nature.*
>
> *In the meantime, every day you're pushed on to greatness, inclined to succeed, on a conscious planet, with inner default settings of abundance, health, happiness, and the ability to manifest whatever your heart may ever desire.*

For a very long time, I preferred thinking it was my journal that answered me, and I absolved myself of all responsibility for what it said. Turns out, the ideas received come from my higher or greater self. A thought that's more new age-y than I like. Some might call it soul-writing, but that's more religious than I like. Apparently, as was just mentioned and as you'll see again throughout the coming pages, there's another part of us that chose to be here, a part that existed prior to our birth and will live beyond our death. And this other part is very much like us, including our personalities. But just as we chose to be here, we also chose to forget where and who we were before we arrived, so that we could be more fully present as who we've now chosen to be! Actually, I think this makes a lot of sense. It means that there is the Mike Dooley I know myself to be and the Pre–Mike Dooley that I know not of, who is still me but with a far greater remembrance of all things. Hence the terminology *higher* or *greater* self, or the perhaps relevant comparison of that part of me to my soul.

These days, I don't think it really matters where the answers come from. It's kind of like having a cosmic ATM that keeps dispensing free spiritual currency. Would anyone really care where "it" came from as long as no one was hurt, misled, or short-changed? As long as the "money" was always put to good use? As long as it never failed? Right?

WHAT IS TRUTH ANYWAY?

Overall, big picture, the coolest thing I've learned from this process, which probably won't seem very cool to you at first, is that there is a singular, benign truth to all things, including life on earth; this truth is attainable, absolute, and objective, and finding it will always afford you maximum leverage on creating major changes in your life. If, indeed, you're someone who has any interest in shaping your future, nothing else matters as much as knowing what the truth is concerning your situation and how life really works. Relevant truths can spontaneously heal and restore, calm and inspire, and help you to laugh more and worry less. Seeking them, however, like creating change itself, is purely optional.

I've sought such truths—as you must have if this book is in your hands—in every area of my life, and in so doing, I've discovered who I am, why I'm here, and all that I'm truly capable of doing, having, and being. And the insights, tricks of perception, and handle on life that have brought me so much can bring you the same.

To my great relief, several characteristics have been shared by all the answers I've received. They've always been logical and intuitive, to the degree I can readily evidence their existence in my earlier life experiences. Fine for me, right? You'd expect as much, eh, drinking my own Kool-Aid, as it were, so let me objectify what I mean. The answers I've received have further passed what I now refer to as my Beauty-Power-Inclusive Litmus Test. They all:

1. *Speak of life's beauty, or*

2. *of our magnificent power, while*

3. *leaving no one, under any circumstances, behind.*

Pretty simple, huh? Can you beat logical, intuitive, beautiful, powerful, and inclusive for determining legitimacy? Seriously? Besides, why would life on earth be hard to figure out? Wouldn't you expect that there are clear answers to your questions, available and knowable by all, that could help people live and love their lives? Why wouldn't they be obvious? These are not rhetorical questions; please suss them out for yourself.

Now, of course, you don't *need* me or anyone else to tell you the truth about life on earth; you can figure it out yourself. And so could you learn to sing like Michael Bublé, spin yarns like J. K. Rowling, play tennis like Roger Federer, or create an empire like Oprah Winfrey, right?

Not that what Roger is to tennis, I am to truth; *knowing the truth about life is fantastically easier than winning international tennis championships!* It's just that my life and bliss have led me to a path of shining a light into darkness.

CONSIDER THE ALTERNATIVE

You'd have to agree that any serious life adventurer, like yourself, *must* either (1) answer such questions concerning *their* life on earth for themselves, (2) accept other people's answers, or (3) abstain. Is there another option? No—my point exactly. So, I want to give you the tools for, and a head start on, drilling down to your own empowering answers, which, because they're objective and absolute, will be the same conclusions presented in this journal, the ones I discovered for myself, as have countless others who have come before us, many of whom are teaching about life, dreams, and happiness to this day.

When people ask the hard questions about life and answer them for themselves, in the privacy of their own minds, using intuition and logic, and perhaps the litmus test above, their epiphanies and discoveries are going to sound very similar, in fact identical, to those of others who have found *the truth*—not because "copyrights" have been breached, but because, again, *there is a* truth to all matters of time and space, and it is always attainable, absolute, and objective.

I'd like to suggest to the skeptic that the truth not being known doesn't stop it from being true, and that just because cavemen and cavewomen didn't *understand* gravity, didn't mean they couldn't observe its effects or deliberately use it—rolling boulders down hills and inventing the wheel.

There is a truth to all matters of time and space, and it is always attainable, absolute, and objective.

Most discoveries precede their scientific proof. Right? In fact, isn't it from observing our lives and the relationship of objects over time, in space, whether atoms or galaxies, combined with intuition and logic, that science receives direction and takes form? Isn't science first a study of effects, not causes? The truth exists before anyone knows what to call it. And this is true concerning all aspects of life on earth.

ON KNOWING EVERYTHING

To qualify my claim of getting answers: my questions usually pertain to my life and happiness. I do not claim to know all things. But I don't think our brains were meant to know everything. They were designed to handle just those immediate things that apply to our lives. Most things, then, ethereal and material, here and beyond, cannot be easily grasped or deduced, such as why there's apparently more matter than antimatter, what really makes gravity work (we still don't know![1]), who you may have been in the 12th century, and why other people do some of the crazy things they do. But, contrary to appearances, most of these things have

---

1 *Einstein theorized gravity results from the curvature of space-time.*

little to no bearing on our happiness today. For *that*, I've found clear answers most certainly exist, can be found, and can be used with relative ease.

Is There a Danger in Speculating on the Nature of Reality?

Are you kidding?! It is, perhaps, our highest responsibility to speculate, weigh, consider, deduce, and thereby know what we can know. Further, the Kool-Aid of "life is beautiful, you are powerful, no one is ever left behind" does not foster devil worshipping or the formation of suicide cults. Beauty-Power-Inclusive Litmus Test fail! Truth remains the common denominator in all of our lives, and given the nature of what's shared in this journal, finding out more of what it is may likely be the surest way to safety, security, and happily-ever-after.

I do not aim to make others wrong or start a new religion, although to be honest, I was afraid you might think both . . . so I asked, and this is what I got:

> *Just as there is no "wrong" yoga pose, because any pose out of balance will end in either collapse or self-correction, neither is there any wrong way to truth. Every road "home" will either get you there or take you to a different road that does.*
>
> *It's fair to observe that all cultures, religions, and beliefs offer noble attempts to understand life and for their practitioners to live well. Yet given the aforementioned, unyielding truths and the hijacking that takes place atop many religions by self-serving and or confused leaders, it's quite common that, in hasty pursuit of their original high aims, they drew assumptions and made conclusions that were in need of some "self-correction" onto more direct "roads."*
>
> *Yet today, as evidenced by the dramatically declining popularity of world religions, most people have understandably grown tired of seeking spiritual truths within their preconceived limits. Its reliance on the belief that truth exists outside of*

yourselves no longer seems self-evident, particularly with your breakthroughs in science. You're ready to go within, no matter how much it hurts at first, and without the need to fear those who disagree. You're ready for the full truth, not vagueness, platitudes, or mere snippets concerning positive thinking, creative visualization, and the "law of attraction." You're ready to learn not only of your power but of your responsibilities.

As these types of dialogue continue the world over, they will put legs under the table for all the feel-good "woo-woo" that's been floating about, so that it can be seen as anything but woo-woo. With openness, the truth alone will urge, coax, and lead you down a path in which you will objectively see the nature of reality, and once you do, you will then have the simple yet necessary knowledge on how to live deliberately, create consciously, and love more abundantly than ever before.

And when you truly "get" that what's offered are not opinions or options, but objective, benign, absolutes that accurately explain your past, present, and future, prepare to be astounded by how your life blasts off.

Our premise is simple:

You are a creator for whom all things are possible, and you create through the focus of your thoughts, your words, and the actions you take—enabling metaphysical principles and an intelligent Universe to conspire on your behalf.

This truth exists whether named or not—believed in, scoffed at, rolled up and smoked. No matter what one's religion. No matter their life path, culture, or traditions. No matter what their parents believed. While every life is experienced subjectively, the stage upon which they're played must remain unyielding and objective, including the outpouring of love that sustains it. These truths are yours to know. Freely available. Yours for the asking, if you ask. And while there's much you cannot fathom of realms beyond time and space, or even within them, there's always enough you can uncover to live joyfully.

Word.

And so, this book is a collection of my questions and my answers, chosen to help you joyfully rock your life. These questions and answers have given me the traction to live deliberately and create abundantly, loved and in love, with lots of friends, traveling the world, living a life that has exceeded my wildest dreams.

I offer it to reassure and confirm *your own* suspicions about life being totally awesome. To goad and love you into the absolute truths that sustain your very existence. And to ignite and inspire a renewed excitement over your own life's adventure.

These pages are not to be the catalyst for more dogma. They don't contain a single rule to follow or to break, and they harbor no hidden agenda, other than spreading some really, really good news about life on earth.

Your brother in adventure,

CHAPTER 1

WELCOME TO THE JUNGLES
OF TIME AND SPACE

Won't people run amok without the fear of God and hell?

Can I still pray?

How could anyone know where to begin on a quest for "the" truth?
Who has the time?

Amen!

Who were the prophets?
Are angels real?

Really?! So, there's no God, like from church? No hell? No devil? No judgment? No consequences? No punishment? Karma?

Do we come back? Is reincarnation for real?

And what about secret societies?
What are they hiding?

Maybe life is better not knowing some things?
Ignorance is bliss, right?

Who has time for this?! How can anyone know what the "truth" is when there are over 4,000 religions?! People have to make livings and support families. Where would I begin?

Everyone has time for this. The upside is insane—dominion over all things.

As for where to begin? Do nothing but ask, *expecting your answer*, and the truth will reveal itself.

It doesn't have to be as hard as you're making it. The predicament you've created for yourselves comes from looking for answers where neither they nor you exist—in the past. As if some story of virgins and prophets and God, or various gods, will give meaning to your life and times.

Do the stories really matter? Of course you've been taught they do, by people who were taught they do, by other people who first told the stories to leverage analogies, devise metaphors, record history, and make points. The past holds important lessons, but do children have storybooks that contain lessons more valuable than what they'll learn among friends and family out in the world? This is not to say you shouldn't read books; just don't think some story about the beginning of time and the origins of the Universe will teach you more than your heart and mind can in the present moment.

It doesn't matter *how* you got here, and, clearly, the mortal mind was not equipped to figure it all out. It is, however, supremely capable of grasping what's now happening in your life, why, and how to change most of the things that displease you.

There is only today. There is only now. You have only to be concerned with, and can only truly know, your own life. Nail it, and you will achieve what you came here to achieve.

Yet . . . if it's a story you want and context you seek, go with one that gives you peace, that helps you frame life's beauty and your magnificent power, and that leaves no one behind.

Such as?

How about this:

Once upon a dream, before this odyssey of life in the illusions ever began, there was you and your best friends, fearless explorers of the unknown, masters of the universe, in fact, but feeling restless, anxious, and just a little bit bored. Whatever it was you wanted, you got. However you wanted to change it, you did. And whatever you wanted to be, you became. Your existence had become so "same old, same old," you hardly felt like the explorers you were. It wasn't enough, you agreed. So being masters, you decided to invent a brand-new dimension.

Suddenly, there was a wide-eyed curiosity among you about who would be the first to leap, the first to forget, the first to kiss, the first to tell, the first to fall, the first to get back up, and the first to remember that it all began with a dare: to love in spite of it all. The probabilities for fun and games were so infinite and expansive that, upon its inauguration, there was a really "Big Bang" that rang throughout eternity.

This new dimension was especially cool because it made possible the previously unthinkable ability of being in just "one place" without being "everywhere else" at once! Of course, you were really still "everywhere else" at once, but now you were actually able to dim this awareness enough to focus on being a single "somewhere."

This may all sound pretty tame, but back then, it was revolutionary. You see, such "separations" from one another had been practically "impossible" because back in the "day" you had all just been "One" and partitions were impossible. Collectively, you were, as is whispered to this day, a "Great Omniscient Deity," or G.O.D. But now, while you were still "One" in this new dimension, still divine, it allowed you to have a totally unique perspective on everything. For instance, you each then had a secret pattern you could follow, among new "heres," to orchestrate your very own magic and experiments, which led to calling your dimension the Secret Pattern Adventure for Creative Enlightenment, or S.P.A.C.E. for short. Now, instead of just "being" the cosmos in its entirety, you could actually travel through it, from one "somewhere" to another.

Soon after, M.A.T.T.E.R. was born and began to fill space as you discovered that whatever you thought about, you brought about, Manifesting Any Thought That Existed into Reality, and as could be predicted, you soon Hid Under Matter Animated in the Now (because time had not yet been invented), playing H.U.M.A.N., and the fun really began.

Ultimately, having all hidden so well that no one could be found, you invented T.I.M.E. to Trace one another In Material Existence, and things got really crazy as you added secret rendezvous and dates to your busy schedules! You then spent so much time in space, hiding under matter, that among various emotions, fear was born, mysteries evolved, miracles abounded, and then, by complete surprise, yet as if it were scripted, you got so caught up in this most awesome adventure of yours . . . you forgot who and where you really were! And to this very day, legend has it that you're all "lost in space" . . .

P.S. Lately there've been rumors of a rumbling in the jungle as you've been growing bored again, this time with the same old patterns and loops you've been experiencing for millennia. The rumors say you've started self-reflecting and wondering in earnest about life on earth, how you got there, how beautiful you are, and how powerful you seem to be. Many are leaning ever closer to remembering the truth, wondering if they weren't actually Born to Expand the Infinite Nature of God, and they're beginning to really dig just B.E.I.N.G. themselves. And so the plot thickens . . .

Sound familiar? It ought to. Welcome to the jungles of time and space! A good kind of jungle. The best. Where the adventure is real, but the lions and tigers and bears are not.

You are, literally, the eyes and ears of "God"
come alive in the dream of life.

Even as you forgot who you were, *it hasn't changed who you are*, always, everywhere at once. Your focus has just become so finely tuned to your creations, you've lost sight of the big picture. Not a "fall from grace" brought on by neglect or arrogance, but more of an anticipated, juicy transition in a fabulously brilliant plan that has made your adventures possible.

You are, literally, the eyes and ears of "God" come alive in the dream of life.

Wait, is that a true story?

What does it matter? Remember the point? It's a story, but one that gives context for what should now be extremely apparent in your life: that the world is beautiful, you are crazy powerful, and in this dreamlike reality, all present are co-creators. *Now you have traction.* Observe your life, scan your past, weigh the future, and witness how awesome you've been, you are, and must always be. Understand the intricacies and nuances of how you created in the past and you will master creating in your future.

That you could even consider this story means you clearly have it in you to glimpse reality in a broader context than most have seen heretofore, until now *thinking life is something that happens to them.* Not. Your innumerable personal triumphs support this. Life is not about survival of the fittest. Come on, you've blown survival to kingdom come! So has everyone else. Against all odds, supposedly. Yet the fact that you're all thriving shows the odds were misunderstood. The real odds are that you, and every-one else, eventually, over lifetimes, will totally rock these gentle jungles, because you *are* the omniscient, unlimited, fun-loving gladiators of the cosmos.

Yes? But blasphemous, you wonder? Get over *that* old story! Feel the presence of truth. Such a recognition hurts no one, cele-brates all, instills confidence, and incites love. It radically changes everything for the better. Life is a banquet. All things are possible. You are forever beings. It's time to stop reacting to your old cre-ations and to start deliberately shaping new ones.

Prior to time and space, you had it all, but it was boring. Then you learned how to *pretend* you didn't have it all, while still actu-ally having it all, so that you could launch yourself into journeys to get what you felt you were missing, thereby following your dreams, in which you would serendipitously fall in love and be loved, time and again, and ultimately experience all that "life" has to offer. *Talk about an adventure! Holy Wizard of Oz!* You just have to "wake up" and the spell will be broken. Even if this doesn't usu-ally happen until you die, at least it will happen, does happen, for all, in realms where the "amnesia" begins to wear off. No matter what happens in "here," everyone returns to "grace" (not that you ever really left it) as more than who they were before it all began. *Everyone wins! Everyone beats cancer! Everyone hits the jackpot!*

Do you understand now, in this new context, that you never would have opted to "play" this game if in any way it meant you could lose? No one would! Even if you had only a .0000000001 percent chance of failure—*no way!* Why risk "having it all," since you did and still do? The work-around, to ensure suspense and therefore adventure, is for life on earth to be so believably "real" that you think a chance of failure actually exists and that such a potential failure might be permanent. Ha! Just like in a nighttime dream, it's because you think it's really happening that your heart starts racing.

By fleetingly, just for the duration of a lifetime, believing that your world is real, all or nothing, you might not only feel fear emerging, you might experience it in humungous proportions. But the same goes for hope, passion, joy, romance, excitement, love, and every favorable emotion ever known, all with a much greater likelihood of occurring because these are in alignment with your very nature and the truth of your presence in the jungles! Hasn't your life borne this out? A thousandfold? Ten thousandfold?! It couldn't be any cooler. Time and space are where dreams come true; where thoughts literally become things when you have the courage and the consistency to think and act on them. This is a where you can go from having nothing to living a life amid opulence. Where you could be alone one day and surrounded by friends and laughter the next. This is where you can discover your power and live pain-free in absolute health. This is where anything can happen and where the distance between fear and triumph exists only in your mind—the greater the chasm, the greater the challenge, the greater the eventual celebration! This is what you, and everyone else alive, *chose*.

Scary! This is also where we might get hurt! We could even die!

Yes, life can hurt. Yes, you might "die." And worse, you might even wish to die yet remain alive, writhing in either physical or emotional pain. But given your heritage, being of God, by God, for God, and given your clearly evidenced resilience through hard times and crises up till now, *you can know* you're bigger than whatever you meet in this dream.

Haven't you, like everyone else, been pummeled so hard you wondered if you would ever be happy again? Haven't you had times when there was no light at the end of the tunnel? Maybe no tunnel to even look for a light within? Yet you rebounded, and the sun rose again, leaving you to wonder, "How could I ever have felt so depressed? Was that even real, or just a dream? Was I serious? Am I remembering it correctly?"

Yes?

Yes! *Remember this the next time fear gets ahold of you.*

This is your life right now. It's a dream. A sacred, precious dream, but still just a dream. One in which you've hidden from yourself your own *awesomeness*, which only adds to the intense drama and romance of every single day.

This is the nature of the winding path making up each life-time on earth. Not because God is testing you (what would be the point?) and not because the devil made you do it (there's no such thing), but because when you're lost in space and know not that you are a creator, feeling vulnerable and at risk, like a statistic not a soul, afraid and hopeful at the same time, you can really, unintentionally, foul things up . . . *causing you to finally seek the truth and crank your life back up into higher realms of love, joy, and learning!* You see, such disconnects, if you've got a curious mind, *are your invitations to reconnect.* And short of fully waking up to the truth (which is not easy, nor necessary, to transform your life), even just partially waking up means it's game on! Party time! Rock and roll!

So there's no God, like from church? No judgment? This sounds awesome, except then, what's the point? What are we really here for?

You wanted to be here for the adventure of it, that's the point, the whole point! Knowing in secret that no matter what happened, all would always be well. And if it wasn't for this secret you even now keep from yourself, there'd be no challenge, and with no challenge, no adventure. And interestingly, both adventure and challenge are products of emotion. Even more interesting, both are the product of desire plus perceived limits.

Desire + Perceived Limits = Emotion = Challenge = Adventure

This is what got the ball rolling in the jungles of time and space, it's even captured in our new, handy story, and it's what gets you out of bed each morning. Desire is a yearning to feel complete when you think you're not. It pushes you to acquire, avoid, grow, stretch, eat, sleep, breathe, and more. It does these things, however, only when you believe in limits.

For instance, without the illusions of time, space, and matter, there's no such thing as "here" versus "there." "Now" versus "later." "Have" versus "have not." But, of course, believing in the illusions, once you find yourself "here," you'd rather be "there"; "without," you want to be "with"; and "present (now)," you can't wait for "tomorrow (later)"!

Because you "bought tickets" for time and space, you also bought a lifetime seemingly shrouded in limitation. Yet here's the rub: even (actually, only) from within the illusions can you go limit-busting—*groove on!* Get it? Again, no limits, no adventure! For example, if you "have not" a home on the water, fabulous romantic partner, or zippy sports car, you can dream and move toward "have." If you are "here" in Florida, you can dream and move toward "there" in London. If you are a student, you can graduate. If you are unemployed, you can gain employment. If you don't like how much you weigh, you can change it. If you earn $20,000 a year, you can earn $200,000 a year. If you are hurt, you can heal. If you are ill, you can become well. If you are worried, you can calm down. If you are sad, you can be happy. If you are happy, you can be happier. All made possible by your belief in the *illusion* of limitation, which brought about the original condition.

Challenges aren't a sign of weakness, but of strength—
evidence that a slumbering giant is about to awaken.

Journeys then ensue as you move toward your many and varied destinations. And it's during the journeys that you love, are loved, and are drawn through all sorts of unexpected challenges (opportunities to grow). Hey, if it was easier, you wouldn't care, and there'd be no adventure; why bother, right? If you already had everything, you'd have no dreams to fulfil. In essence, you have dreams that will take you to places you've never been before, starting from a place of disappointment; otherwise, you wouldn't be dreaming them. Right? But going where you've never been before requires living through what you've never lived through before and being who you've never been, hence the unexpected challenges. *"Huh?!* I'll have to speak in public in order to share my insights and tap into my greatest gifts?" *"What?!* I'll have to be disciplined and determined to write a book?" *"Seriously?!* I'll have to love myself if I am to be loved?" *"Really?!* I'll have to treat my body responsibly if I'm to be fit and look fabulous?" *Ugh!* But in doing these things, you become more than who you once thought you were.

If you think about this, it's quite logical. All dreams come with built-in challenges, and all challenges come with built-in dreams—overcome the challenges and live happier than you were before they arrived. Now, using your skills of observation, you can reasonably deduce that since this applies to everyone, it's very likely the way it's "supposed" to be in time and space. And so, *this is, at least in part, why you chose a life on earth.* And it means that challenges aren't a sign of weakness, but of strength—evidence that a slumbering giant is about to awaken.

The observable progression of every life on earth:

1. Believe you are a limited being living a chance life in a finite world.

2. Feel angst and desire from an ever-present sense of incompleteness.

3. Soothe the angst by following your heart, moving in a new direction, and doing new things.

4. Discover weaknesses you didn't know you had.

5. Press on, improve, strengthen, rise above, and banish weaknesses.

6. Watch dreams come true. After which, you're like, "Of course, I rock. Ain't no thing."

7. The cycle continues, and after repeated successes, you realize you're an *unlimited* being in an *illusionary* world.

8. Grasp your divinity and that of all humanity.

9. Move on to new frontiers, realms, and dimensions, or go back to help others learn what you learned, or both (after all, you have the "time" and you can be in more than one place at once).

So, long ago, I knew it all, then I chose to forget it all, so that I could remember it all? But if knowing all is so great, why'd I choose to forget? Maybe my life is better not knowing some things? Ignorance is bliss, right?

Just because you chose to believe in the illusions doesn't mean you don't still have power over them. And while that power may not be enough to fully transcend them, you hardly need to in order to manage them.

You didn't come here to master walking on water or levitation, although both are possible and will eventually be done. You came here for the entire bold experience of being human, which you're handily fulfilling. Yet anyone who'd optionally like to maximize their joys and minimize their sorrows, without undermining their human adventure, simply needs to clue in a bit more. The closer to truth, the more abundant, friendly, and joyful your life. The farther from truth, the broker, sicker, and lonelier you'll be. Curiosity and a quest for knowledge will reward you handsomely.

Every civilization has therefore sought greater wisdom to live better lives. Everyone is born wanting to know what's going on. Your mind was once hungry and inquisitive, but you were shut down, told that "All of the answers lie with an angry God." Or "Such answers can't be known by human minds." Many societies believe that a mere presumption that you *could* know such answers, or even just having the audacity to question, evidences your weak and sinful nature, precipitating bad karma and a fiery, long-term stay at Hotel Inferno. So, of course, you stopped asking questions, and *there went your power.* Except . . . the questions never really went away, did they?

Happily, you are indeed bigger than whatever and whoever you've met in this dream. Your flame still burns brighter than you realize, and, if you so choose, you can use it to connect stray dots, reconcile loose ends, and make meaning of the beauty that motivated those before you, who sought the truth but believed not in their ability to receive it.

Concerning the purported bliss of ignorance, look at it this way: The potion that makes medicine "go down" smoothly, the medicine that might otherwise cause you to gag, is called an *elixir*. And the elixir for all that may ail a life on earth, which may also be quite difficult to take, is *understanding*. Understanding *truth* is pure power. Not understanding, maybe thinking that God decides things for you; or thinking that your lucky stars must line up; thinking that a black cat or walking under a ladder or a poorly executed ancient spiritual contract can jinx you; or thinking that maybe you're supposed to be poor in this lifetime—all these needlessly rob you of your power.

Even in the absence of understanding, civilizations still prosper—so great is the human inclination to succeed. Yet think of what life on earth might be like once everyone achieves clarity about life's beauty and their own power. Confidence and optimism will soar! Dreams and desires will take root! Everything will seem easier! Cooperation will flourish! And trust, faith, and love will blossom in ways unimaginable today. This is what understanding promises.

Understanding means getting rid of the garbage, the self-doubt, and the belief in your vulnerability. It means no longer thinking a God outside of you decides, passes judgment, or gives tests. It means realizing you're a spiritual giant and you have the power to shape and direct your life as you joyfully choose. It means letting go of dogma, the past, and societal beliefs that never felt right; it means the end of blame, of excuses, and of the belief that there are victims. *This is exciting!*

Bad stuff? It happens. Evil people? They abound. Are you a creator? *Yes!* And should bad stuff or evil people ever cross paths with you, gifts will be exchanged, there will be order, there will be healing and love. And while no explanation will ever be great enough to put a "happy face" on the many sad things that happen in the world, nevertheless those things *do* have explanations that include, at a minimum, the thoughts, beliefs, and expectations of all involved. There are no victims, only volunteers. And the fact that this is almost impossible to see at times doesn't mean you can't sense it is true.

If we're all making this up and it's all our imagination, why can't we just change our minds to change everything and blow this Popsicle stand?

You can, but do you really want to? You may think you do, but that you live and breathe today has meaning. You're here because you're still choosing to be here at the very deepest level of your being.

When "blowing this Popsicle stand" is truly what you most want, you'll be gone soon enough. Not spontaneously, however. It may take a bit of time; you bought that ticket, remember, abiding by time and space? There must be order. You have other desires as well, and there are seven billion other co-creators alive today, which must be considered, as paths are woven together and apart.

There are no victims,
only volunteers.

It's often stated that "everyone gets to pick their own truth." Sounds so loving, yet a slippery slope it is. Sure, everyone gets to pick, but picking a "truth" does not make it true, for them or anyone else. The truth is the truth. Gravity, for example, affects everyone the same, no matter what they "pick." And while everyone gets to order their own dessert at the local diner, they still have to pay for it.

When you see others creating their reality in the same time, same space, and upon the same earth as everyone else, doesn't that imply there must be certain absolutes, parameters, boundaries, making it possible for them to create their own reality while still sharing it with others? Mustn't everyone—doesn't everyone—clearly share certain inviolate, immovable commonalities?

There are, indeed, particular, concrete principles and rules that all must share and abide by, which create the stage you now live your life upon. Call them pillars of reality, parameters for living in the jungles of time and space, or absolute *"truths of being"*—greater than the earth's known physical laws, which are actually quite malleable and relative (you'd be surprised). There are certain truths upon which the physical world is nestled that are so immovable, they will prevail in every life *whether or not you even believe in them.*

If you didn't have such absolutes, then anything could happen next. A chandelier could turn into a car; elephants could turn into sparrows, people, mountains, oceans; or the planet might suddenly, unexpectedly, and for no apparent reason disappear. There must be some minimal, dependable, base, blank, smooth, unchanging "fabric" for time and space to exist, in order for you to, individually and collectively, print your "design" upon it.

Recognizing these pillars of time and space, which are child-like in simplicity and in full alignment with the Beauty-Power-Inclusive Litmus Test, is powerful, not just for what they are, but for what they *are not.* Understand that these, in effect, are your only true "limitations" within time and space, yet they enable far more than they prevent. And within them lies the latitude and full range of movement for all to achieve whatever they set out to achieve with their life on earth.

THE "TRUTHS OF BEING":

1. All are One: of One, of God, Divine, interconnected.

2. Thoughts become things: Everyone is a Creator.
    All are God.

3. Life is eternal: Life = Consciousness, God, energy, you, yourself.

4. There is only Love: There is only God.

5. It's all good: Everything is exactly as it "should" be; there is order, perfection, and love in all.

You can live your life with blinders on, or not. But imagine living with the realization, for example, that what you do to me, you do to yourself—compared to not knowing this? Compared to thinking that whatever you can get away with doesn't count?

These truths reign over your awesome, beautiful, entire existence, giving you a stage to play out your adventures upon, instilling you with power, and providing a common thread with all of the other actors who've agreed, like you, to act in this time and space. Choose to see the obvious, without a fight or resistance, and suddenly there's clarity. You can go forward and deliberately live the life of your wildest dreams without worrying about judgments, mistakes, lost opportunities, or other lies that you'd believe if you didn't know any better.

What about secret societies? What do they know that we don't?

These are simply membership groups concerned primarily with their spiritual views, which were highly unusual for the times in which they were created because originally their views were all about *life is beautiful, people are powerful, and no one should ever be left behind*—clearly a threat to any church that relied upon the fear of God to subjugate the faithful. Well-known secret societies include the Freemasons, Skull and Bones, and the Rosicrucians. They've always existed through exclusionary policies—to do otherwise at the time of their founding meant certain death—and to this day this is neither wrong nor improper; all are free to gather, socialize, and celebrate among like minds, and all are free to decide whose minds are alike.

Chief among their aims, naturally, was the preservation of their treasured worldviews, passing them on to successive, carefully chosen members over time. And such preservation efforts were to one day pay grand dividends when their "secrets" could safely be shared with inquiring minds the world over, to no doubt spark a spiritual revolution that exalted life on earth.

By now, however, so much time has passed since most were founded that even though many embrace camaraderie, community, and service, their original reasons to be secretive have been lost and forgotten.

"Spiritual, not religious"—not just for dating websites?

While religion was your first foray into spirituality, metaphysics was your first foray into science. In the beginning of every quest for truth, religion and science typically start out holding hands, asking, "Who am I and how did I get here?" Yet both religion and science remove humanity from the equation, as if humans were irrelevant, afterthoughts, secondary to life itself.

Spirituality is the human recognition that there's more to reality than what the physical senses detect. It's the awareness of a supernatural intelligence, of which you are part. The awareness that there's order, meaning, and love behind all; that there's good everywhere, in everyone, and in everything. The awareness that you are eternal, powerful, resilient, and here to joyfully thrive.

Aren't there consequences for "poor" behavior?

The only real sin is not seeing the truth about life's magnificence and your own beauty. And this omission of sight is punishment enough, without any need for a make-believe devil in a nonexistent hell. Think about it: What could be worse than living in paradise, where your thoughts become things, you are loved and adored, and everything is possible, yet not knowing these things and, therefore, not experiencing them?

What about Karma?

Karma, believing that what goes around comes around, is not an absolute law, but a phenomenon, albeit a very common one. If it were a law, it would interfere with the immovable "pillar" of thoughts becoming things. Similarly, it's not a scoring system, as in, if you violate 15 times you will be violated 15 times.

It means, however, if you choose to live in ignorance—thinking, for example, that violating people is sometimes justifiable (for *any* reason)—*then you will live in a world where others think the same*, and violations will be considered an unavoidable part of life.

What breaks this cycle, like any cycle, is enlightenment. Understanding life deeply enough to realize that violating others, to use this example, is *never* a solution. In the moment you grasp this, you are off that "wheel," no matter what the score.

Can I still pray?

Please! Prayer is beautiful and powerful because:

- The person who's praying obviously believes there's more to reality than meets the physical senses; there's a higher realm or power to pray to. And such a belief opens the door to such.

- It demonstrates a belief that the one doing the praying has a supernatural connection to that realm or power.

- It's inevitably sparked by *love*, whether that love takes the form of compassion, concern, desire, or fear.

What's not so beautiful about prayer is the old-school view that God is *out there* listening. That He is going to decide whether or not to grant the wish. Presumably based upon whether the one doing the praying, or the one being prayed for, is "good" and deserving. *As if* God lived outside of you, *as if* God needed your prodding to act, *as if* God would ever withhold love, healing, mercy, or whatever was being asked! Fortunately, no such God has ever existed.

Prayer gatherings *are* powerful, not because God is impressed with how many people might be calling for help, but because so many people, moved by love, are directing their attention to a cause, a person, or a challenge with the aim to cure, heal, improve, or surmount. Thoughts that can then more easily become things, for the emotion stirred and the cumulative energy created by working together.

So who were the prophets?

Prophets in any tradition are simply wise, tuned-in people, usually with lots of prior lives under their belts. They are summoned, as you might imagine, when the masses, perhaps driven by suffering, are seeking *and believing in* a better way. Correspondingly, such prophets have a longing to serve, in conjunction with their own life lessons and adventures. They appear not because God sees the suffering and says, "You all could use some serious help," but because the yearning, thoughts, and expectations of the masses fit like a puzzle piece with the yearning, thoughts, and expectations of a wise, tuned-in person (or people), and these thoughts become a "thing."

And what of the angels?

An angel is any conscious being (animals qualify) deliberately giving comfort, guidance, or love.

All people are angels. And there are angels in the unseen. Your religion or lack thereof is unimportant to them; they are happy to appear in religious garb or as ghostly silhouettes, as necessary to match your expectations. There are indeed hierarchies and classifications among them, not as in "better," but as in "farther-seeing and greater-knowing," and some are "responsible" for others. Their success in reaching you and making a difference is greatly helped or hindered by your belief in, and hence receptivity to, their existence.

Important to know is that angels can't live your life for you nor make your decisions. They can, however, through love, reach you, as if whispering into your ear, walking with you hand in hand, smoothing your ruffled feathers, offering bridges as you lean, stretch, and traverse rocky paths and step through tricky situations. And, thereby, they can and do make tangible differences to life as it unfolds on earth.

Are you seriously going to tell me there's no heaven and hell?

Fiction and fiction—at least in the forms they've been taught. You already live in heaven with your life on earth, and there are countless other forms of it, within and without the jungles of time and space. In realms beyond, word descriptions utterly fail. For example, there are more colors than your eyes can even register. More beautiful sounds, tantalizing aromas, and love unimaginable. And yet there are abundant servings of all of these now around you, certainly in more than sufficient proportions to make for a very happy life.

Beyond locales, heaven is "peace of mind" and "love in your heart," and when these are diminished in any degree, you begin dabbling in sort of a self-made purgatory. Not arising from any form of celestial judgment, but from confusion and misunderstandings—which can be banished with truth.

Which means there's no devil or demons?

Neither has ever existed outside of your own mind. Of course, people do dastardly, evil things, but the important distinction to understand is that evil does not exist as a force of its own. Any idea to the contrary is illogical and unfounded. Even ugly deeds done by people are driven not by evil, but by confusion. And confusion can be healed.

Do we come back? Is reincarnation for real?

Yes and no.

"No" because time is illusionary, and the prefix in *reincarna-*tion implies a return. One can't return, or leave, without relying upon time measurements. In ways unimaginable by the human brain, all time, and hence all lifetimes, are happening at once.

"Yes" because *within* time, before and after most certainly do exist. Within the illusion of a single lifetime, you experience a sequential, chronological childhood, teen years, and adulthood. Similarly, beyond any lifetime, yet still within the illusion of time, you then make choices based on lessons just learned, as you set out for another round in "the jungles."

Hip, Hip, Hooray—no judgment day! But won't people run amok without the fear of God and hell?

There is no judgment day and there never will be. You are one with God, and God has no need to judge God.

Why be good? First, it's in your nature. Second, because any deviations from your nature, which can only come through misunderstandings and confusion, as just explained, will cause your life to spin out of control. In times of chaos, ask new questions, and the answers they summon will swiftly guide you to a life of creativity, fulfillment, and happiness.

The truth is, you are magnificent, gorgeous, supernatural, and all powerful. Your thoughts have always become and always will become the things and events you experience. It doesn't get any better than this. Living your life on earth, in the jungles of time and space, couldn't be any easier than getting what you think about. All you have to do is learn to think new thoughts and think them so often that they propel you into action, in a responsive world that loves you. And then, literally, heaven will be seen at your feet, exactly where it's been all along, exactly where it is right now.

CHAPTER 2

The Evolution of Consciousness

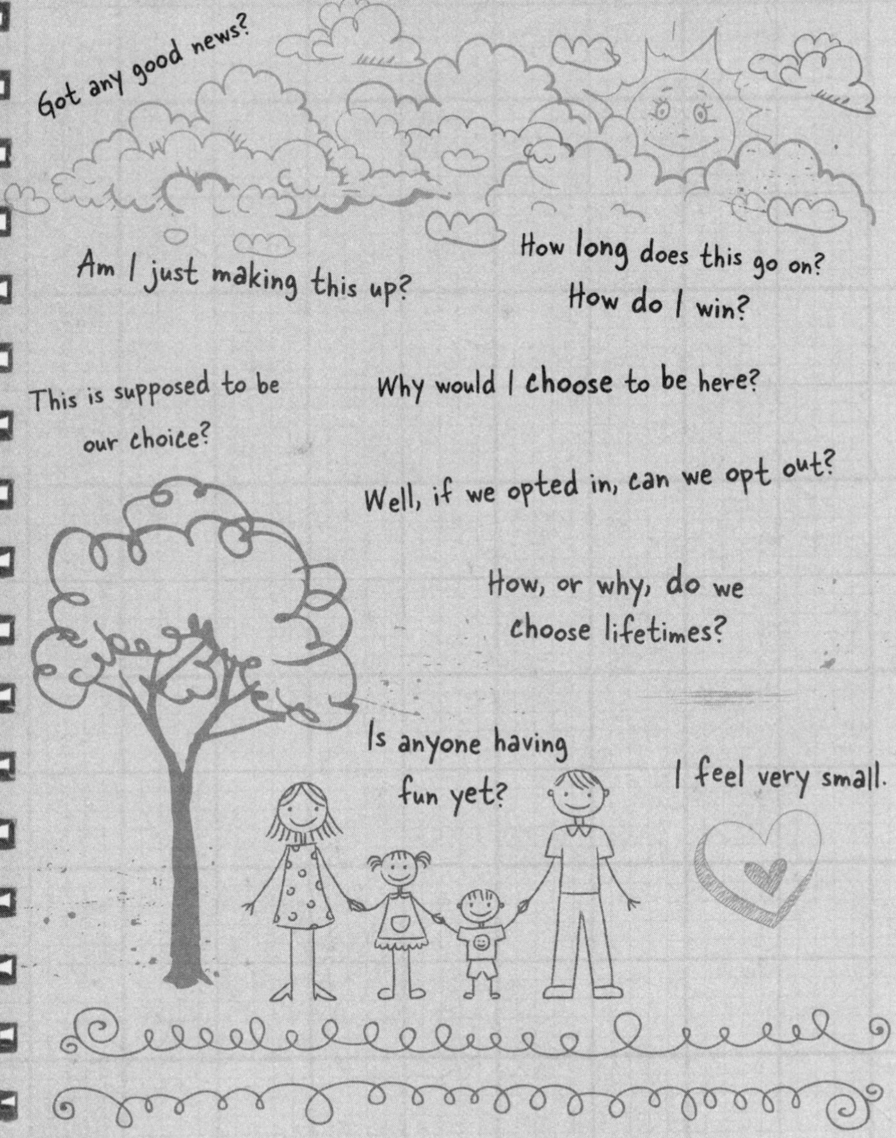

WTF?! These are huge ideas! How do I even begin to understand them?

As esoteric as this topic may seem, if you can get a handle on the simple basics concerning the nature of reality, as if from the perspective of a child—like who you are, why you're here, and what happens next—you'll far more easily live in the moment of each day, enjoying the gift of your life.

What You Can't Know: *Most Things*

Since your brain is wired for the illusions, in fact *of* the illusions, designed for interpreting the illusions, you can't expect it to understand all else beyond the illusions. It's a bit like wearing blue-blocking sunglasses that accentuate wavelengths at one end of the light spectrum and block the other end, and then wondering why you can't see anything blue. With a material brain designed to see, judge, rate, love, or hate the illusions, it is virtually impossible to see and explain the greater reality from which all illusions emerge.

Then, considering the size of your brain in relation to the size of the illusions—including a cosmos made up of at least 10 sextillion stars, and factoring in that your planet alone has millions of different *species*—at best you may only ever know very, very, very little about very, very, very little.

What You Can Know: *More than Enough*

So, to postulate about the nature of reality and what Divine Intelligence may have been thinking in creating these jungles is *virtually* impossible, while also potentially arrogant, deluded, and laughable. Virtually, as in, "almost, but not quite." Which is to say, *your brain can* nevertheless deduce and conclude, with supreme confidence, certain teeny-tiny yet absolute truths (shared with you in the previous chapter) concerning your existence that will

not only empower you but enable you to live a happier, more ful-
filled life from this day forward.

**If we're not here to grovel before God, but to simply "adven-
ture," as you put it, isn't this a bit shallow? Shouldn't we at
least be serving people? Aren't we here to know love?**

Nice! The fact that you've even asked implies you're beyond
thinking your existence is some weird cosmic accident and you
understand there's intelligence in the world.

To answer the question yourself, because it's a far easier one
than you presume, just look around the world today and see the
commonality in all lives. Beyond surviving, can't you see what
everyone is truly living for? Isn't everyone engaged in *the pursuit of
happiness*? And that's it: the answer that's vexed and evaded overly
analytical minds since the "beginning" of time.

HAPPINESS VS. LOVE

Of course, you could say that people the world over seek to
love and be loved. They seek food. They seek water. They seek
sunlight. Many seek to be of service. But all of these things are to
ultimately make possible the pursuit of *their* happiness.

---

*Your lives are not about love, they are about adventures
into love. Your adventures are the variable, not love.*

Love is not the answer, as many suspect. Love is a given in
your experience, like the air you breathe. You didn't choose to live
in time and space for air, for example, any more than you chose
it for love. Time, space, and love are merely mediums that make
your lives possible. This isn't saying love isn't vital, nor that it's
not supremely necessary for your existence. Like air, it's both.

That you exist at all, living and growing nearly *effortlessly* upon your oasis in the cosmos, means surely you come from pure love, are now bathed in pure love, and will return to pure love. Anything less than *pure* would imply the perfection of the cosmos was not perfect at all. And why love? Look at your power! Look at your beauty! Look at your freedom! Look at how deeply you are allowed to love and be loved! Seriously?? Is it really necessary to prove love when you get to live so blithely upon your giving, lush, beautiful, abundant, symbiotic world, where, somehow, in spite of yourself, you continue to thrive?

While you may want to be more aware of this love or you may want to channel it in greater measure, such ambitions would always be to further your adventure, learning, and the pursuit of your happiness—not for love's sake. There's no such thing as "for love's sake." Divine love simply *is*, without grade, pure and unrelenting.

Your lives are not about love, they are about adventures *into love*. Your adventures are the variable, not love.

THE MAKING OF ADVENTURE REQUIRES A SENSE OF INCOMPLETENESS

As was lightly touched upon earlier, you can also observe that all adventures, 100 percent of the time, are made possible by a perceived sense of incompletion, leading to a host of more commonly known ailments, such as feeling inadequate, being intimidated by a challenge, struggling with adversity, conjuring fear, and similar difficulties.

This inherent sense of incompletion is actually a trait of the immortal. It's the inherent condition of wanting stuff you don't yet have or getting rid of things you no longer want. More precisely, your life on earth is made up of chasing things you pretend you don't have—love, friends, and abundance—while worrying about things you pretend you do have, like problems, challenges, and issues. Until one day, you happen to notice the prophetic powers of pretending.

This is your *Divine Sense of Incompletion*. It is evidence of the presence of greatness, proof that divine consciousness is present, and it doesn't ever go away. It's among your greatest gifts; it's not a curse and it doesn't mean you can never be satisfied. Satisfaction can come *in the pursuit* of your desires and needn't be delayed for their manifestation.

Feeling incomplete derives itself from the intersection of desire and your belief in time and space as reality. The moment you decide you want something, it's always because you *think* you don't have it. Of course, this is what starts adventures and gives you reason to arise from bed each day. And, of course, given your awesomeness, you will get that which you are desirous of; yet you'll find that once you do, or even while still in the process of getting it, you'll have settled upon something else you want (that you think you don't have). Again, this condition never goes away. Hallelujah! This is fantastic, unless . . . you're putting off your happiness until you feel complete—because *that* ain't happening. That misunderstanding can lead you into a serious funk as you erroneously believe that you'll never get all you want, or that what you want is not meant to be, or that you are somehow flawed.

Why not choose both? Embrace your "incompleteness" as you simultaneously strive to become more each day, and in the process, grant yourself permission to be happy?

Why and how did I supposedly choose this life, and why and how will the next one be chosen?

You can only go so far "back" in answering "why's" because eventually they will, theoretically, bring you to the origins of divine awareness, or God, at which point the question will fail because "origin" implies beginning, which implies time, which is an illusion. Yet for every other "why" before you reach that limit, the answers are deducible, observable, and always the same: *because you chose to, because you wanted to, because it was fun (directly or indirectly), because you are a natural-born adventurer.* Just as these answers clearly work for explaining the vast majority of decisions made at the crossroads of every modern life on earth, so are they the rationale for all decisions that came "before." As to the admittedly sad, uncomfortable lifetimes—for example, those spent amid disease, abuse, or war—while you can't see their reasons, you can similarly deduce that such reasons nevertheless exist. That there was order, purpose, and love involved. You can also understand that the suffering was and is extremely brief in comparison to eternity (not that this justifies it or makes it seem remotely acceptable). And you can see that such lifetimes represent small exceptions to, not the rule of, life on earth.

For explaining the "how" of each lifetime, the steering mechanism is simple: TBT—Thoughts Become Things. Just as your thoughts become things in this world, so did they, and do they, before and after each lifetime. You'll be the same "person" after this life—though perhaps wiser for the wear unless you've been subjected to sustained fear and dogma—and the afterlife will offer you an improved perspective, guides, a reinstated memory of other lifetimes, and more, all combining to elevate your vantage point. The *countless* reported near-death experiences of your fellow life adventurers clearly confirm all of this.

You are a massive package of energy, passion, and fear, all of which will still be very real at the time of your passing. To the degree the desires, fears, and expectations you held in this lifetime are unrealized, unless your new vantage point warns or enlightens you away from them, they'll lead you to "choose" your next step and to craft your next lifetime with the leanings, traits, and inclinations that are most likely to yield whatever you're still after.

Who or what was I before my material incarnation? What do realms and dimensions look like before and beyond time and space? How did God emerge to "be"? Where did God come from?

The world, or dimension, *immediately* before and after this one is also made up of illusions of time, space, and matter, although far more malleable. You didn't just choose to be who you now are; to even have such a choice arose because "earlier" you wanted to adventure in the time-space continuum, which inevitably meant having many lifetimes to choose from, as well as all the "spaces" in between such lifetimes. Such "spaces"—in which you process what just happened and plot the probabilities for what will be next, still thinking like a human and needing all the same reference points—are also, necessarily, framed by these more malleable forms of the illusions.

Concerning the world, or dimensions, "before" and "after" time and space? Let it go. Remember, "here" you can know very, very, very little about very, very, very little. The answers to these questions will never be crystal clear from within time and space, but here's the great news: any questions you can't answer are irrelevant to your happiness today.

Go with what you know. That you are alive now is indisputable. The important question, then, is really, "What are you going to do about it?" Sure, context may be helpful, raised by exactly these questions, and should be sought when possible; just remember that your focus for now is on interpreting your illusionary world *from within it*. Which is like a fish born in and living its life in a fabulous, million-gallon aquarium while wondering about life beyond. That "beyond" is truly incomprehensible; if you try to wrap your head around it, you will have little traction. Instead, learn your feeding times, warm spots in the aquarium, light patterns of the day and night, who your tank-mates are, and the various nooks and crannies that have been placed in your home by a well-meaning owner, and you will at least make the absolute most of tank life. Which is exactly "where" you are with your life on earth, even though you can also surmise that it's very, very, very likely (given the phenomenal order seen throughout your world and among 10 sextillion stars) that *awesome, mind-bending* objectives are being met, which *will* "one day" make perfect sense once *all* of your lifetimes are complete and you return to "whence it all began."

You are here, period. Wake up, discover, celebrate, rock on. So what if you now have little idea of how or why you got in your "tank" and no idea of what will come next? Through observation, you can see that you will nevertheless call this place home

your entire life. You can notice that you are phenomenally powerful, that what you resist persists, and that what you think about,
you bring about. That the energy moving you is free, that love is
everywhere, that those sharing your space are as awesome, scared,
and hopeful as you, and that your "tank" *is* a blooming paradise
of splendor, beauty, diversity, simplicity, complexity, and abundance—all quite indescribable. Your "tank" is actually more like
a gigantic, whirling, living, loving sphere . . . called Earth, that
constantly provides for you. This is not an accident! *It loves you.*

Be here now.

Everything will make sense when "all my lifetimes are complete"? What or who is the determining factor for completeness?

You have no doubt heard the expression, "That person's an old
soul." Not unlike references to "baby souls." As usual, such nomen-
clature has a greater meaning than is normally understood. It
implies that in between "baby" and "old," there'd be other stages,
too, like "young" and "mature" souls. The implications are spot-
on—just as the physical body moves *and grows* through stages over
time, so does the "soul," or call it the energy essence that is the
sum total of all your lifetimes, including the earlier part of you
who chose to venture into these jungles and have all these lifetimes. Unlike the physical body, however, which ages and passes
through these stages in a single lifetime, souls grow more slowly,
over multiple lifetimes. You carry with you, from lifetime to lifetime, all the wisdom gained in each, cumulatively, yet with no
clear memory of the lessons or the events that imparted them.
This is to ensure that in each incarnation you are more fully present as who you have then chosen to be than you could be if you
were trying to hold space for everyone else you've been!

To swing this into another orbit, just as physical bodies and
spirituality predictably evolve, so does the collective soul age on a
planet. To simplify, you could also say that at any given time in history, there's an average soul age of all the participants then alive.
The tricky thing here, in part due to time's illusionary nature, is

that everyone doesn't start out at the year "dot" as a baby soul—some will choose to start out much, much later. You can just as easily choose a date in the future for your first incarnation as you could choose a date in the past to be an old soul! Yes, choosing to go back in time for a future life may alter one or more concurrent, parallel versions of the future, but we'll save that theory for another day.

Thus, there will be planetary inhabitants of various soul ages at any given time, and the collective soul age will then, for the most part, progress, chronologically, with increasing maturity, into the years, centuries, and millennia "ahead." Consciousness upon a planet, then, logically, progresses similarly to the consciousness within an individual's soul, which progresses similarly to that of the physical body.

Hypothetically, speaking generally, a planet's "first" soul inhabitants will be mostly "babies." A few mature and possibly some old souls will also show up to offer guidance, if they aren't killed off for being too different. As in the world today, people prefer to be with others who are like-minded, even if they are baby souls. Then, just as a body ages, even though time is an illusion, so will the population, over generations, mature. Before long, with fire, metal, and mating under their belts, yet perhaps with emotional matters still in a fuddle, they'll start building and aiming nuclear weapons at each other. Older still, and they'll realize that not only are they powerful, they are also responsible for how they use their power. Shortly thereafter they'll discover the Divine dwells within all, yourself included. Eventually they find life is a self-created gift—by God, of God, for God—that all things are possible, thoughts become things, one's "beingness" is eternal, there's only love, and it's all good.

Knowing of this evolutionary inevitability is how your ancient prophecy makers, Nostradamus included, from many thousands of years ago, were stunningly able to predict where you'd likely be in your spiritual growth right about now, including the consequences of your likely choices. They were picking up on the probable trajectory, the anticipated metamorphosis of your evolution as you became more than you've ever been before, to this day, crossing a threshold that humanity has not yet crossed on planet Earth. And obviously, predictably, they foresaw not only your growth and expansion but the angst and resistance that would accompany your ascension, the likely planetary chaos stemming from your inevitable growing pains.

So where are we on planet Earth in terms of being a young or old civilization?

Young. Immature, approaching early maturity. Not unlike an individual's late teenage years. Hormones firing. Nice guy, bad girl, sneaky, tricky, pouting, demanding, forced to swiftly learn how to inhabit the body and realm of adulthood. It's a whole new world with different rules, expectations, and a playing field different from anything you've previously experienced.

Naturally, you need some time to connect the dots after any transition, especially as you grow into having more responsibilities. At first there's denial. Things were pretty cool "before," and you were getting stronger and more powerful every day! You went from learning how to push and shatter your limits to suddenly having to learn when to impose them, upon yourself! Now there's inner angst. And like all feelings, which are simply emotionally charged thoughts, this angst will seek expression in your life, in concert with all of your other thoughts and feelings. Such angst may eventually manifest in terms of anger, arguments, fights, confusion, accidents, sickness, dependencies, acne—the possibilities and mutations are endless. And all the while, thoughts become things. Your happy, bouncy thoughts and your angry, fighting thoughts compete for their own expression on earth.

But just as teenagers can't refuse to physically grow up, neither can anyone refuse their spiritual evolution. Individually and collectively, here on earth, right now, the march continues. There's no turning back. Resistance is futile. Yet, for those who don't grasp this, who hold on to old ways and conventions with clenched teeth and bared fists, tension will mount.

Nothing, in fact, can, has, or will ever happen upon the face of your earth that isn't first ordained in the thoughts of the population upon it. Collectively, for example, intermingled with your planet's gentle consciousness, you and your fellow human beings create the weather. All of it. You're not bystanders or mere witnesses. You actively, directly, create it, 24/7. It's a mirror, as is every*thing* in time and space, of what's going on within you. Not to overlook seasons, cycles, patterns, and physical laws, which powerfully enable the weather—*except you create those too*. Not only thunderclouds or sunshine, but tornadoes, hurricanes, and, similarly, plate tectonics and earthquakes. Remember, it's all illusions, your illusions, and in this case, your collective illusions. And for all the collective manifestations that were set into motion before your birth, and still having chosen to be "who, where, and when" you now are, no matter how the world looks to you today, trust you knew exactly what you were getting yourself into and it suited you perfectly.

You went from learning how to push and shatter your limits to suddenly having to learn when to impose them, upon yourself!

Now the baton of creation has been passed, as you ride upon the momentum that suited your own lessons and growth, and everyone alive sharing the planet has stepped into co-creator roles.

But I don't know anything about meteorology or plate tectonics! How could I influence them?

Everything that happens on your planet is tied to the feelings of the people on it, and it most certainly doesn't matter that this seems *not* to be true. You don't remember beating your heart? So what! When does remembering something have anything to do with its legitimacy? Besides, it's not supposed to be so obvious; it's supposed to seem "real"! Only then can you forget you're dreaming and be driven by your passions and emotions so that adventures and journeys can follow. Just as in a nighttime dream, everything seems real—game on! There's gravity in a nighttime dream, right? There may even be a thunderstorm or earthquake, right? And *in* the dream, they make sense. There are reasons, there may even be weather patterns, heat, evaporation, downpours. Wow, nice manifesting! But once awake, no one ever doubts that they are the creators of their nighttime dreams, including the gravity and weather within them. There's also no doubt your dreams serve some purpose. And that the purpose is served by the dream *seeming real*. *Voilà*, life on earth!

Everything defined by the illusions is part of the dream you're now having, and to any degree you share an experience, which means sharing illusions, like the weather and plate tectonics, you are its co-creator. And, as always, you create from the inner world of your thoughts, beliefs, and expectations the outer world surrounding you.

So, when there are inner storms of angst, there will be outer storms upon the planet; when there is inner calm, there will be outer calm. Happily, you can eventually control any outer storm by controlling the inner ones. *Which is really exciting.* Because not only can you learn to quiet the world's chaos, you can learn to direct your creative energies toward discovery, awakening, peace, and love.

To begin this, you must let go of what served you in the past, learn how to have traction in a world you thought was happening *to* you, and realize that all along you were, and still are, happening to *it*.

OK, I need a reason to believe all of this. Where's it going? Does anyone win here?

Everyone wins.

To put all of this into context, the endgame, for having taken the plunge into a life on earth, is simply to live it as joyfully as possible. As stated, this is already what everyone's life is now about, whether they admit it or not. You are alive to follow your heart in every major direction it pulls you, thereby forcing you to face every beast that rears its head on your path, ultimately delivering the greater YOU to a point of divine higher-vibrational satisfaction—serenity.

Not a serenity that comes from laziness or from a life toned down by fear. But the kind that leaves a huge smile on your face, peace in your heart, and acceptance for everything, everyone, and everywhere. The feeling that you could happily live lifetimes on earth forevermore. Understanding that it's all being played out in God's hand and that all are where they most want to be, living the greatest adventure ever devised by Divine Mind, where every wrong will eventually be made right, and all lies will be made whole. And then you may have reached the "end of the game."

Hmmm. I've met many who've told me that if they have the option, they never want to come back. Can they opt out?

You simply cannot wisely choose to opt out of an incarnational adventure based upon *the vantage point of your mortal life* because, for example, you've had a bad hair day, month, or decade, or because you've stubbed your toe, slipped and fallen, or far worse. Too much is being done by and for your greater self to pass judgment on the choice to be in this incarnation while you're still in it.

In other words, taking into account the totality of your being, your greater self *and* your mere mortal self, once your incarnational adventures have begun, your greatest desire will always be to see it through, even though during some low times within a lifetime, the mortal experience could be pretty miserable.

Remember, that you are now here has meaning. Wanting to exit early neglects that for your presence in the "jungles" today, *you're actually still choosing to be who you are.* Besides, consider this shocking twist that arises from time happening simultaneously:

since time is an illusion, the choice to even visit the jungles begins *and ends* in the same "instant"! Once you choose incarnational adventures, in that "moment," you've gone and come back, been there, done that, all of your incarnations. So at what point in that instant is the question supposedly showing up about the whole thing being a bad idea and you wanting off?

So, to back up again, where are we in terms of the lessons we're learning?

Collectively, the weighted average soul age on earth today is about that of a 21-year-old. Of course, some are far older, and some are mere babes. But the weighted average would be about 21. You're therefore living among people with lots of energy! Lots of excitement! Lots of frustration! Lots of angst resulting in lots of ugliness, but far more hope resulting in lots of beauty. Spirituality, without the need for religion, is at last blooming, along with the requisite acknowledgments and deep understanding of your power and responsibilities, leading to a realization of your divinity.

Well into discovering your power, the task now at hand is understanding the responsibilities that come along with it. Beyond tackling the more common and base energies of discrimination, scarcity, and a false sense of your vulnerability, are the trickier hurdles now before you, which lie beneath words like "blame," "fault," and the whole concept of victimhood. No conversation of spirit can hold these failed notions. To harness and use your full power, you must accept full responsibility for everything in the past and present. If not, if there's a belief that "things" can somehow just happen to you, accidentally or through divine intervention, then *that belief* alone will make it true. Without such misunderstandings, nothing can stand in your way.

To ease you into this, understand that accepting full responsibility for everything in your life does *not*:

1. deny you have been violated,

2. condone or justify such behavior,

3. rule out any of your options for recourse, or

4. mean you have to understand, other than very generally as we're now doing, *why* you experienced whatever you experienced. Forget "why." It hurts too much, and asking will simply keep you from being present and looking forward.

Accepting full responsibility does not mean that what happened was *your* fault or you were to blame! These words fail no matter where the finger is pointed, including at yourself. They imply a context that does not exist. They imply recklessness, intention, and failure. Nonsense! You are an adventurer, inspired into action for the fun of it, doing your best to learn and grow, an eternal being. Everything that happens, therefore, adds to who you are and who you will become. Everything that happens expands what God is. There is no failure when you are still in the game, doing your best, getting better, learning, and growing, which eternal beings forever are.

If in your creating, manifesting, stretching, reaching, and growing, you draw someone into your life who violates you, lessons will be learned so that such connections are not made again. Nevertheless, if there were indeed someone in your life who acted "against" you, you would be the reason.[2] You are the cause of everything you experience, whether or not others participate in your manifestations. Understanding the deeper reasons for such experiences, why you created what you created, will come in time when you're ready, in some cases only after the physical end of this lifetime. Meanwhile, for all things that have ever happened, you will want to cultivate a sense of, "Yeah, I had a role in its co-creation." Perhaps adding, "I don't know what that role was, nor why I experienced it, but I know I live in a world of order, healing, and love, and one day it will all make sense." This is how to

----

2   *Publisher's note: much more on this sensitive topic appears later in the journal.*

increase your vibration, rise to a new level, and move into power like you have never known before.

You're asking a lot. What if I, or "the people," resist these changes of consciousness that are happening on the planet?

You and they *are* resisting! Which is natural and expected. These new thoughts can take some getting used to. They hurt, embarrass, and can even humiliate. Accepting responsibility might even undermine an entire lifetime of excuses and justifications that someone could "safely" hide behind. But the truth is the truth, and to resist it means to live in contradiction, which will always be far more calamitous than embracing it. It sometimes takes many lifetimes of denial before you understand this. In that time, your manifestations will be all over the board—good, bad, and ugly. You'll believe, you won't, you'll blame, you'll cry, you'll feel powerful and powerless, and you'll continually give your power away until you claim it back through understanding the truth. Ultimately, the price of resistance is far higher than acceptance, which is something everyone has to learn for themselves.

Throughout this period of growth and resistance, the earth will continue spinning as old systems (of religion, politics, economics, etc.) begin to malfunction and either evolve or completely break down. And in the unlikely scenario that resistance continues, your collective survival will be powerfully tested, though not through some sort of Judgment Day, but because you'll have denied nature and yourselves the chances to rectify imbalances. In this case, your civilization will join the long list of other dynasties, kingdoms, and empires that came before you, only to "disappear," leaving in their place myths and vast ruins that litter the world, including Atlantis and ancient civilizations of Egypt, Rome, Greece, China, Turkey, and *hundreds* of other sophisticated sovereignties of which you know nothing. The reason each and every civilization before you disappeared had nothing to do with the floods, wars, earthquakes, or plagues that may have seen them off, but everything to do with the thinking that precipitated such floods, wars, earthquakes, or plagues.

Those souls of fallen civilizations continue on, of course; many are among you today, trying again, and others have been drawn to different times or other planets, where the collective soul maturity *is in resonance with theirs.* Win-win. Everyone has a place to go to live, learn, and adventure that matches their vibe. Any attraction to false ideas or resistance to truth, as well as the resulting chaos, will persist until the one clinging finally begins to consider, "How else might I view this?"

You are creators, consciously and deliberately, or blindly and in ignorance—it matters not.

Kind of handy, huh? Want to know if you're in alignment with truth? Ask, "How's my life going?" The bumpier, wackier, and more riddled with mysterious disappointments, the more you're "missing" the truth about who and where you are.

Got any good news?

That's it! You're receiving it now! Others are too. People everywhere *are* waking up. Never before in history have so many human beings been so concerned with the environment that even some of your giant, multinational corporations are investing vast fortunes to clean up past disasters and to ward off future ones. Never before have so many people clamored for and insisted upon common decency and respect to prevail in the world. Never before have life spans so consistently risen, as well as standards of living, upon every continent. Times are fast changing.

You need only try, incrementally testing the truths that your open heart and mind, and those of your fellow beings, are now attracting, thus bringing this present civilization to heights that earlier ones couldn't have imagined for themselves. For in merely trying, you evidence the belief that life holds more for all of you and that you are capable of uncovering it. And such beliefs, combined with such action, are all you've ever needed to transform and revolutionize life on earth.

Where do I start?

Lean in. Given what's logically and intuitively important, a civilization's degree of evolution can in large part be defined by the degree to which it cares for *all* of its individual members. Not selflessly, but in your own best interest. Yet on earth, caring for everyone has been hard to do, if you don't first love yourself.

It's time you understand and celebrate the importance of the individual—every single one, no matter who they are.

You've all been overlooked, *by one another.* You've been asked to sacrifice, be selfless, and to put the needs of others ahead of your own. You've been told that your leanings to indulge and be happy were caused by your animal nature. You've been taken advantage of by leaders who were either lazy or greedy, and you've been taken advantage of by each other.

The rationale has always been that if everyone works selflessly, the society will grow and make for strong individuals. This is actually the exact formula for deadening one's spirit and negating the very reasons you chose to live upon this bastion of perfection in the cosmos: to be you, to be free, and to see what might happen. You sensed and knew that strong *individuals* would make for strong *societies.*

No one's to blame. You thought your leaders' ideas made sense and you played along, giving away your power. But enough is enough; it's time to celebrate your individuality and follow your heart and encourage all to do the same. This is the epitome of being self-responsible.

- Honor Yourself

  Honor and respect yourself and all of the dreams you were born with. These aren't yours accidentally, but are gifts from your higher self. They're part of the very reasons you chose to be alive now—to make them come true. Your dreams are yours to remind you of what you're truly capable of doing, and the joy you'll find as you move toward them, into adventures of both love and hard lessons, will make you a light unto humanity.

- Love All

    You can't properly honor yourself without automatically considering others. If those in your life are hurt or unhappy, how happy and free can you be? Love others, not only through empathy, and not only because they too are of God, but because you love yourself and their happiness will help lead to yours. You're getting this now.

You are who God most wanted to be,
here and now.

Which does not mean yielding to everyone. It doesn't mean you have to keep anyone in your life you don't wish to keep in your life. It doesn't mean you have to spend time with those who've disappointed you. Understand that nothing you could ever do will ensure another's happiness; that's up to them. You don't owe anyone anything greater than the happiness you owe yourself. And understand that if someone is now on your path, it has meaning. A meaning that you get to carefully assign and define. Maybe they've showed up as an invitation for you to find strength sufficient to ask them to leave!

So when does God reenter the picture?

God never left. God is present, *through everyone.* Life on earth is happening *inside* of God, inside of creation. God is here experiencing it, perpetuating it, creating it *as you.* You and your fellow beings are each a mini-me of the Most High, not apart but *a part*, using the power of your thoughts, words, and actions to further life on earth. And the implications are, quite obviously, staggering.

You are alive on earth to decide . . . EVERYTHING. You *weren't* put here to be tested, judged, and sentenced. You were not an afterthought; you were the first thought. You are not an accident. Nothing, therefore, has been left to chance. There've been no mistakes. You are eternal. You are all powerful. You can do, have, or be anything. And as to why you're here, as implied and stated already: you *had* to have chosen it. *You had to have.* You were not assigned here. You are not an infant, virgin baby soul. You're an ancient gladiator who existed before time and space was ever thought of. You are pure God. And God doesn't go where God doesn't *most* want to go. Which conversely means something stunning: you being who you are is not only what *you* chose and most wanted, but you are who God most wanted to be, here and now.

Yeah.

This is who you really are and how you got here. Rest assured, all is supremely well. You knew what you were doing when you chose as you did. You might not remember why you chose as you did, but you can know that you did, and that the decision had to have been made from the epitome of your brilliance, for gorgeous, wonderful, loving reasons that made flawless sense from *the zenith of your majesty.*

Sound far-fetched?

If so, ask yourself, "What's the alternative?" There are only two main schools of thought that now commonly answer that question: One says you're here randomly, by chance, a total freak of reality, without reason, order, or purpose. The other says you're here because "God" put you here to see if you're ready for heaven.

But wait. Revisit our "new" idea that you're literally the eyes and the ears of the Divine, one with all creation. Doesn't that make sense? Doesn't that honor everybody? Isn't that fair? Doesn't that jibe with the power you know you wield? Don't you feel you matter? Don't you know you're brilliant? Haven't you always done your best? Hasn't everyone? Haven't you sometimes felt you would utterly burst with the love you felt for another? For a pet? For yourself? Even though many questions may be pouring through your head right now, even though you may feel some initial resistance (that's what we've been talking about), overall, yeah, you as a God-Particle makes way more sense than any other explanation. Life is beautiful. You can feel these ideas resonating. You're a truth barometer, and you get excited when you hear what you know is right.

How much farther do we have to go? Will the day dawn when everyone is having a blast? Are we having fun yet?

Earth is on the verge of the most exciting time in its history. About to cross a threshold that's never been crossed before. About to offer its inhabitants what it's never offered before (thanks to its inhabitants): to be alive at a time when the light of truth will overcome darkness. This has never happened. You are a pioneer of spirit, alive in a world of your own creation.

You saw the opportunity for adventure. You chose from an infinite number of possibilities. You considered Stone Age living, futuristic cloud-top living, and then, "Look!! Here!! The end of the dark ages at the dawn of first light, on a super-rich, rocking, bountiful planet! One that has remained absolutely gorgeous and thriving, in spite of prior irresponsibilities! Sign me up!"

You are a pioneer of spirit,
alive in a world of your own creation.

You're still within your civilization's redemption period, *as you knew you would be*. It's not too late for the greatest of comebacks; it's already begun, humanity is waking up, asking new questions, and very little "work" has to be done, other than the modest changing of a comparatively few minds. The effects will snowball. Momentum will quickly gather. Change will be exponential. Even now there's wealth and booming economies the world over, in spite of their fragility, yet still nothing compared to the land-of-plenty where you're headed. The simple, obvious realizations already shared can give you peace, putting you in a place of power, moving you away from hopeless, disempowering mantras, like "I have no idea. God must have put me here. We are all victims living in a cold, inhumane world." Instead, "Oh my gosh! This is our chance to wake up to who we really are and live like we've never lived!"

The truth is you do live in a dream world, and in a single lifetime, rather than many spanning millennia, you can move from the darkness into the light and understand that you are your dream's weaver. Yet there *does* remain this choice. You *are* at a crossroads. Which will you choose? To awaken or resist? Therein lies the suspense, adding to the adventure, adding to the fun.

CHAPTER 3

The Matter of Illusions and the Reason to Care

Who cares?

What matters?

I wanted to believe in lies so that I can learn the truth?

What's important?

I'm finding this disturbing . . .

Should we forsake technology?

If this is all a dream, who would want to be me?

Dream

I mean, if everything is an illusion, why bother?

Drama is more important than technological breakthroughs?

What if I don't care?

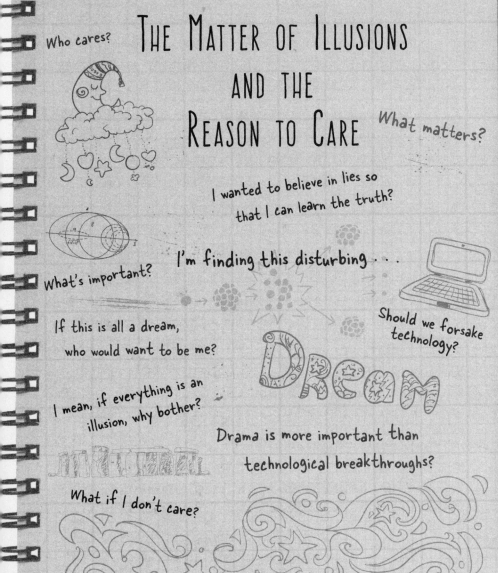

Who cares? What matters? What's important?

Loath to gall you, but cutting to the chase . . .
Nothing and everything.

To be more specific, nothing matters, but everything's important.

If you think this is playing with words, saying something and then seemingly negating it, playing both ends to the middle and being safe, *know that even without the latter half of the sentence, there remains an immovable truth: Nothing matters. Period.* Which, to point out the obvious, runs the risk of sounding rather defeatist. Really, who needs to write in journals or read books if this is true?

But whether or not something matters depends upon it making a difference. Right? Whereas whether or not something is important depends upon value. Hang on . . . and maybe read that again.

WHAT YOU SEE

If the context in which you process most things is—we are physical beings alive on earth for a short time, in the depths of space, upon a linear time line—then to you, "Nothing matters" is likely the most absurd, counterproductive, idiotic thing you've ever read. And this would be true whether you believe in God's grace (making such a declaration frighteningly blasphemous) or you believe life sprang from some random, cosmic "mistake" (equally frightening).

If this is your context, then to you, right now, *everything* matters, *desperately matters*, and everything has profound implications in terms of both your immediate survival and any long-term chance you might ever have, "chance" being cruelly literal, of finding happiness.

WHAT THE TRUTH IS

Alternately, having gone within and asked the hard questions, as we have been doing, and then deducing just a little, you realize:

- That everyone comes from and returns to Divine Intelligence, Source, God.

- That everyone is a spark of God, having created the here and now for the journeys it would afford; for the sheer, raw experience of feeling alive while living shoulder to shoulder with death. To learn, to discover, to adventure, to love *as if* it were optional. And "afterward," you will all still have forever and ever as you expand eternally, metaphorically in the palm of God's hand.

- That you exist independent of time and space. Time just marks where you think you are in the creation of your present space. Similarly, matter isn't real, it just shows you what you've been thinking. Both arise from you; you did not arise from them. Yet because of your beliefs (or misbeliefs) pertaining to them, of "where" and "what" you think you are, feelings and emotions arise, and BINGO—the very point of the illusions is achieved!

- Further, if all are individually and collectively creators of the illusions, this means you came first; you came before the illusions. Therefore, truly, life is not happening to you, you are happening to life. No matter how things may ever appear, nor how surprised you are by them, you are actually projecting them, not perceiving them. Time, space, and matter are all illusions. So even a zillion years from today, you'll still have a zillion more to live, and more after that, and then eternity after that!

This leads you to the stunning conclusion that whatever happens in your life on earth, or in any other quarter of the physical universe, in any year, including this year, *doesn't matter!* Because you will still, always and forever more, be *you*. You are greater. You, your identity, your soul, are real; all else is not. From this perspective, the perspective of truth, transcending the illusions, *nothing matters.*

"Oh, no!" "OH . . . YES!"

Yep, this perspective is at once both disturbing and exhilarating.

The immediately awesome implication of nothing mattering is, as you say, "out of this world"—far, far out of this world: *You never again have to worry about anything, ever, no matter what.*

The trials and tribulations, accolades and triumphs happening right now in your life, upon your planet, in every land, among the poor and the rich, between races and religions, in the end they may as well just be nighttime dreams for all the effect they have on "forever and ever in the palm of God's hand." *After all, they are, in fact, just illusions!*

Time just marks where you think you are in the creation of your present space. Matter isn't real, it just shows you what you've been thinking.

In the sense of things mattering as you have always thought they do, they don't. Yours was just a perspective brought on by believing that the illusions were "real." More to come on this shortly. Which is not to say that you won't have preferences on how your days unfold; you mostly certainly will. Again, hang in there, lots of elaboration to follow.

Yet because, obviously, you chose to be here, and because, obviously, a purpose is being served, and because even though whatever happens won't, can't, diminish or tarnish your greater essence (the spiritual you), we can still say that whatever happens or doesn't happen has value and is thus *important.*

But if something is important, it matters. If it matters, it's important. I think you really are trying to hedge your bet, which is quite annoying.

This is not about splitting philosophical hairs. Consider, by any old-school definition, things that "matter" matter *because they can change outcomes*. Right? But do you get that nothing can change the outcome of you being you, eternally, powerfully, gorgeous, loved, and forever? To understand this, you must simply cease associating your identity with your physical body and realize that you and your personality will survive its physical demise. It's not like when you die, your personality dissolves into some vast greater self, like a cube of sugar in hot water. While you may more clearly be one with your greater self at that time, your transition won't require a loss of identity. Why would it? Even now you live your life and think your thoughts "inside" of God, yet without losing your sense of self.

Yes, you *could* say that if something is important, it therefore matters, but wouldn't it be fairer and more accurate to say that since nothing matters, nothing is important? Hard to swallow, but yes? Although saying so would make it far more difficult to have the discernment we're trying to achieve that will lend itself to living one's life deliberately. It *is* fair to recognize that even though life is a dream, within it you still have preferences and things you value. Just as you might value the inspiration from a nighttime dream while still recognizing that what happened in the dream itself was make-believe. Similarly, time is just an illusion, but *within it* it becomes something you must deal with, manage, and consider; it becomes important.

Similarly, again, Hollywood movies both educate and entertain, but does the movie itself matter? Are people really killed and are hearts really broken? Are there really victors and villains? What's achieved by the viewer is *important*, but not so much how it's achieved. *Just like life*, so vivid and real. Except as supernatural beings, *the thing you may choose to understand*—oh, boy—is that there's always an infallible safety net beneath you.

So, "I am" and will always be, no matter what, no matter what, no matter what?

That is the distinction worth getting here, because again, there is a profound upside:

The "you" who you treasure most, whom everyone loves and treasures most, and everyone *you* treasure the most—you're all indestructible, intergalactic, immutable, forever-and-ever beings! Impervious to circumstances! Untouchable by mortals! You are a celestial given! You will always be! You and your loved ones can't be lost or become less through what happens in, or even *beyond*, time and space! You are all of God, by God, for God! Nothing in time and space matters, because in spite of the infinite possibilities that truly exist for all manifestations, there's not a one in which you won't prevail, rise above, and soar far beyond.

Feel the relief? Feel it now. *Go rock your life on earth!*

All return "home," whole, complete, richer, and wiser for the wear. Salvation and jubilation for everyone. It's a win-win-win-win-ad-infinitum situation. There's not a single loser, contrary to what your physical senses show you. "Bad" things simply do not exist in the jungles of time and space when you stand far enough back from the equation to see everyone emerging from every situation as more than who they were entering it, which is equally true of entering and leaving *every* lifetime.

None of which is to justify or shrug off the hideous and inexcusable things that certainly do happen within the illusions. These create huge emotional adventures, and they are, therefore, extremely important. Again, now, you see a distinction emerge between the drama and trauma versus what is real, and this distinction should ideally be maintained to keep perspective, have proper context, stay sane, and maximize your adventures in joy.

Yes, coolness, except one thing: the bad guys still get to run amok!

Not so fast. While you do indeed live in a dream world where, in the long run, every egregious violation and repulsive offense dissolves into nothingness, ultimately adding to who you are, on an adventure in a world where all (the violator and the violated) are assured of "winning"—the violator still has to "pay the piper." Due to life's utter transparency (you all being of One) and given that everyone survives *everything*, by the time your amnesia wears off, there are no secrets! Meaning, no bad deed goes unrecognized (by everyone); no one gets away with anything.

---

*Truly there is nothing quite as fair
as life within time and space, more
exacting than rocket science will ever be.*

The logistics are quite simple: Consider that everything happening on the planet happens because of you or one of your neighbors, because a spark of God created/perceived it. Wouldn't you fully expect that everyone is either aware of, or capable of becoming aware of, all things? Of course.

Meaning, all offenses, even little ones, that you and countless others silently suffer in a lifetime are known. Conversely, your own seemingly invisible and unappreciated (by others) strength, grit, sacrifices, fear, bravery, confidence, timidity, determination, and heroism become known by all. Truly there is nothing quite as *fair* as life within time and space, more exacting than rocket science will ever be.

All the petty, backstabbing, two-timing, cheating, lying con-artists, who seem to be, if not literally in some cases, getting away with murder, while their popularity and bank accounts soar, will be found responsible for every slight, backhand, and trick they ever performed.

Relief times two.

Your true, often unwitnessed goodness will escape *no one*. Including those who never believed in you. They will see how wrong they were.

So, indeed, *all* lies are eventually revealed and *all* skeletons must sooner or later come out of every closet. In fact, there's not a single secret *you* now have, sorry to be the one to tell you this, that isn't or won't be known by all. Mind you, most will not even care, as they'll be dealing with their own junk. Everyone, to one degree or another, has led challenge-filled lives in which corners were cut, from which a few awkward lessons were learned. And all such learning, by everyone, will also inure to the benefit of all, for the same connectedness—nothing is wasted.

In your life today, worry not that there may be immoral or unethical deeds or behaviors that seem to go unchecked! No one is being fooled. No hurtful behavior is overlooked. Let the victors of any war or dispute write their silly history books, as they have no effect on truth. Such tomes will sooner or later dissolve into dust, leaving behind the ever-enduring "fossilized bones" of truth for all to see. Everyone is found out, even though perhaps not as quickly as those violated would like, yet they will be, in divine ways, as if by divine order. It is simply the nature of your reality, and by extension, that of life on earth.

This is all true, not by "design," per se, nor through any sort of celestially ordained justice. Everyone is simply learning and doing their best. Everyone is an adventurer, cut from the exact same cloth. Everyone already ends up in la-la land forever and ever. Yet you can be comforted, if necessary, knowing that every wrong against you shall be revealed to everyone involved. Everyone's role, whether heroic or demonic, blatant or secret, will be studied. Every listing ship is righted. No longer can it be naïvely thought that bliss may be found in ignorance; you live your lives in Divine Mind, where ignorance has always been a stranger.

And the catch? The slippery slope? Where's the bomb in the gift-wrapped box?

You've been steeped in old stories of life being hard, that it's a test, and God is angry. Told that the dichotomies exist so that you can learn what you like, as if the world was filled with 50 percent good and 50 percent bad, a minefield of good luck and misfortune. Where every good thing comes with a debt that must be paid.

It's not so. You were led astray. The world and your life are 100 percent fan-f*cking-tastic! Come on. See it. You live in a realm where—astonishingly, miraculously, and utterly impossibly—*nothing* makes you less and *everything* makes you more. Do you see? The beauty? The perfection? The genius?

Would you expect less from "God"? Think that through! *Of course you wouldn't!* But do you live your life this way—as if *nothing* makes you less and *everything* makes you more? Do you allow it to add to your joy? Are you finding unending reasons, every day of your life, to celebrate, give thanks, and smile at strangers?

It's time to relax, fear less, be present more, and rock the living daylights out of each precious moment you have. Everything happening is doing so *inside* of a shared dream. It's not about what happens, by whom, to whom, or why, as much as it is about the fact that it happens, how you chose to feel, what you'll choose to create next, learning from those choices, moving through those feelings, and deciding where your journey will go.

It's time to relax, fear less, be present more,
and rock the living daylights out
of each precious moment you have.

None of which is to imply that anything can happen to anyone! All manifestations have meaning and offer much to learn concerning your power and its use. The "whys" behind every second of your life boil down to your thoughts, your beliefs, and your expectations. Accordingly, as you witness your life unfold, you will have the option to see patterns, and in doing so, you will learn.

Thought is life's only variable. *Your* thoughts are *your* life's only variable, choosing them from a palette of infinite possibilities for what comes next and how you'll emotionally react. Drama rocks! Drama teaches! It could be factually stated that drama is the very reason you're alive. Again, not for what happens, but for the fact that it does, the way you sparked it, and how you reacted to it; to give you a measure of your likes and dislikes, highs and lows, loves and loathes. To ignite emotions that *do not exist when you're "everywhere, always, at once."* This is why there's time, space, matter, you, them, here and there, have and have not. These otherwise unimportant distinctions fill you with desire to complete what seems incomplete, sending you into the world on adventures, resulting in *drama*.

Creating intentionally and mis-creating unintentionally, you emotionally experience the concepts of justice and injustice, recognition, values, morals, propriety, respect, pride, and human love. All of which are teaching you how to aim and use your perceptions and perspectives, and all of which appear in spite of the unshakable divine love that holds your productions together, which is as absolute as time is illusionary.

Drama is good, until it makes you unhappy. At which point, eventually, you'll clue in and learn not only how to change your feelings but also how to keep from repeating prior "mistakes." Then you're off "that wheel," with an elevated perspective, gathering momentum, and an upward spiral begins.

Well, actually, I'd like to rock the living daylights out of my life. You're on a roll right now, but what if you're wrong? Or, if you're right, are you really sure I can't screw this up?

You don't get too bent out of shape over your nighttime dreams, do you? You can't really *get those wrong*, can you? Worst case, you're going to wake up and, after a quick panic, think to yourself, rejoicing, *"Oh, thank God! It was just a dream!" None of it matters* for its effect on your waking life—except that maybe there were lessons learned, through simulated circumstances that created drama, that will apply to future waking circumstances . . . *Hey!* Exactly the point! Your nighttime dreams enrich your waking "dream," just as a physical lifetime enriches your greater self; nothing matters during these elaborate productions, except that you go, play, learn, and love, and you simply can't *not*!

And what if I decide again that I don't care about any of this? Why bother?

You do care! You're asking these questions. You've never stopped asking questions. Why bother? Because it's fun! Admit it, it's fun!

For example, even as much as you want to deny truth when first found—"No way! I would *never* choose some of the things that have happened to me!"—you'd still fight tooth and nail to keep this very life should it somehow be threatened. And whatever unpleasant thing has happened to you, you'd rather (not always, but mostly) remember and grow from it than permanently erase it from your life. Plus, you have to admit, it's fun to feel *justified*, eh? It's fun to feel *proud*—of family, nation, *your* life—right? To be bent over in *desire*, fists clenched, pleading "to heaven above" to quench your life's deepest thirst? To know such *joy* that a sense of weightlessness overcomes you? To feel such *sorrow* that it draws you into realms of love previously unknown? To know *passion* with such intensity that you want to surrender into it, be lost, disappear in its ecstasy?

Again, the trick is learning to manage your life's drama so that it maximizes your happiness and minimizes your unhappiness. And as a natural-born matter manipulator, you could not be better equipped to do so! Don't like something about your life? *CHANGE IT!*

You're not meant to endure unpleasant emotions, but to change them. Learning how to create, change, shape, and reshape *the illusions* that gave them rise! When things happening around you begin to take on an urgency that brings you down, it's time to recalibrate. Sure, there's value in momentary sadness and grief—they help you to know the full spectrum of feelings—but wallow not, and refuse to let these mere steps blind you to the golden stairway to heaven you are now ascending. Feel them and move on, change your focus, craft new circumstances, find your power.

None of this is meant to convey a message of "Nothing matters, so why bother?" or "Nothing matters, so don't try," or "Nothing matters, so don't care." The message is that the illusions of time and space are just illusions, and so if you're stressing because of violations or a sense of injustice or whatever to the point of your unhappiness, realign yourself, and thereby your thinking, and thereby the illusions on the stage of your life. The journey and the drama are important, and over these you have total control.

This is almost disturbing. The drama's important? Our inter-pretations and the subjective are important? These are just in our head! Comprising ever-changing, wispy, wafting, often pent-up, sometimes dark, unpredictable thoughts! How can that be what it's all about?

Think of it, before there was time and space, Divine Intelligence was everywhere, always, at once. God, therefore, never knew or experienced what separation was like. Never knew the sadness of a farewell or the joy of a reunion. Or the uncertainty that comes from pending decisions that have mutually exclusive outcomes. The drama! So God, now, as you, can know these things.

For you to discount life now because it's all about the intangibles of drama and interpretation . . . excuse me, but how does that change anything? Before, you thought the material world was hard, cold, and physical; now you're understanding that it's all projected thought. So what? You felt better about crying over spilt milk when the spill was tangible than you do now, knowing it's all a dream? Knowing what you are learning, you can flip this and feel the opposite! Feel better about whatever has disappointed you in life, because "it" wasn't real! The truth is that material things have only ever had a value because of the emotions *you assigned* to them. Life has only ever been about emotions. Yet now, if you can glimpse:

1. What's important is how you, and others, feel—everything else is just a crutch, prop, or excuse.

2. Material things are thought forms and, therefore, can be changed with your mind.

3. You are of God, by God, pure God with dominion over all "things," and you are here by choice.

Then you will:

4. Begin valuing the journey more than the destination.

5. Adventurously set out to change certain areas of your life.

6. Know that everything's always been and always will be A-OK.

Yet, obviously, as we progress as a civilization and continue expanding on behalf of God as you've said, we will naturally discover more and more valuable technologies that will ultimately improve life on earth, giving greater and greater importance to that which you now say doesn't matter . . . right?

The apple didn't matter for Adam and Eve, did it? It was just a prop in the garden, as the metaphoric story goes. A prop, like all props, fictional or non-, that gave them the opportunity to make decisions by how they chose to react to it. The apple itself didn't matter and neither does the stuff that's in your life today, whether you're driving an old Ford Pinto or a brand-new Rolls-Royce. It's all relative, transitory, fleeting. These things can come and go, yet what remains? What will be their common denominator? YOU, and not the physical YOU, the energetic, spiritual, eternal mass of thoughts that claims to be you. "Stuff" is not important, except that it gives you the opportunity to make decisions, the opportunity to choose how you'll behave, and the opportunity to learn about yourself—your power, connection, divinity, preferences, strengths, responsibilities, emotions, and your divine, eternal nature. The "thing" that's really, really important, however, as far as your life, lessons, and love today, is:

That you are here.

The rest of what's happening on the planet, including the degree of technological advancement, is unimportant, so long as you have the "space" to grow and flourish emotionally.

To illustrate, let's just say that in your next lifetime, you will "have to" live in a very, very primitive part of the world. Superficially, from today's perspective, you'd likely be very disappointed and feel great resistance. "No heating? No air-conditioning? No social media? *Really?*"

But if your best friends from this life would be there, and any of your old "lessons in love" would carry over from this lifetime into that, and your hard-earned wisdom and acquired skills would carry over, too, and if your dreams of success and appreciation that didn't manifest in this lifetime would likely come true in the next—*you'd suddenly be stoked!* You'd happily resubmit to a new dose of amnesia and not remember a single thing of this life or its technological superiority.

The illusions, which don't matter,
spark journeys that do.

Do you see? The drama will pick up in your next lifetime, exactly where it left off in this one. The drama is what's important. Your emotions and your feelings are real. The rest doesn't matter. The props all fade into the background, relative, and if you were to go back to the Stone Age or even to 500,000 years into the future, *it wouldn't matter a lick, in the grand scheme of things!* What's important is all that you fear, hate, and love. What's important are the invisible and intangible "things." It would not be about whether you drove a spaceship or a brontosaurus.

Surely this life has already shown you that the thrill of your new car vanishes faster than its new-car smell, rendering it "just a car." Same for the new house, the new vacation, flying first class, eating organic food, claiming the new partner . . . they all fade. Which is not to say they don't rock—most of the time. And it's not to say that you won't have strong preferences. And that flying at the front of the plane is much more comfortable than flying at the back. But such differences are negligible compared to falling in love, and they'd disappear if you didn't first know/remember they existed—just like you don't now miss space travel at the speed of light while in your bed, snug under the covers.

See where this is going?

All that stuff in your life, virtually *everything* that you usually think matters, often to the degree that it can make you unhappy—like air-conditioning when yours is broken, or the theoretical importance of cheap energy for poor nations, like where you live, your career with "Acme Company," the profession of XYZ, how much money you have, the type of car you drive, where, when, and how often you vacation, and so on—*don't matter at all!*

It's time to see the obvious, to tone down attachments to or insistence on having material things, whether they're supposedly lifesaving necessities or luxury indulgences, tools or toys. *Not because you can't or shouldn't have them; you should and you can! They're easy to get when you go within and metaphysically "work it"!* But because they're so incredibly unimportant, not to mention illusionary, *they should not be allowed to detract from your happiness.*

The illusions, which don't matter, spark journeys that do. No matter what time or era you live in, it's basically all the same. Whether you start out on a poor planet with poor surroundings or an opulent planet with luxurious surroundings, all that's really important is that there are "things" you want, from which your one-of-a-kind journeys into emotion will soon follow. Which is why you wanted to be you. Which is why God wanted to be you.

So we should forsake technology? The Amish have it right?

There are no "shoulds." Just "what ifs." That's why you are here. Your life is the biggest "what if" of all. Technology is neither good nor bad, until you say so, or until you choose to pursue and/or use it to your advantage or detriment. The question here is about being responsible with your power and its use when delegated to machinery, inventions, and innovations.

Your "what ifs" may include parent-child and child-parent bonding, sibling adventures, and family love. Community cooperation. Social interactions. Patience, creativity, self-growth, self-discovery, self-love. These are the juice of life. Beyond the material basics, like home, food, and very modest comfort, all the rest, emotionally, can still be experienced. It doesn't matter how people start fires, flicking a Bic or rubbing sticks together, right? It doesn't matter if there's online education or schoolhouses with only chalkboards. You're still going to be born of parents, grow up in a community, embarrass yourself occasionally, learn of your power and responsibilities, support yourself, engage life, be yourself, pride yourself, and learn to love yourself. Don't quite get it all done this lifetime, you'll come back for another round. Blow up the world because of greed or stupidity, you'll dream up a new one. Harness cold fusion? Eh, maybe. Eat with a fork? So what. Smash atoms? Big whoop. Roll wheels down hills? Only if it's on the way home.

Nothing is destined, free will reigns, the variables of every lifetime, based on your thoughts, run the gamut, including when you'll fall in love for the first time as well as which technology your civilization may harness to do its heavy lifting. The first is important, the second only counts to the degree it helps with the first.

Once again: technology is important only when it aids your emotional journey. And in this regard, you "need" very, very little beyond fire. Oh, sure, more technology can be fun! And fun is extremely important. But if in your pursuit of more fun or even of life's necessities, you unnecessarily risk your health, friendships, and love, priorities have been misplaced and you could royally screw things up. Which, actually, has been done many, many times before you by earlier "lost" civilizations. Their inhabitants recklessly charged ahead in the name of progress, losing sight of why such progress was valued, losing all they treasured most.

By looking back and seeing the evidence that litters the world of earlier civilizations and their mastery over the elements, while simultaneously noticing their absence from the world's stage today, you can grasp what went wrong, learn from their folly, and make better technological choices yourself, to the great advantage of all life on earth.

So, basically . . . this brings us back to believing lies in order to learn the truth?

Maudlin, but yes, if you wish. Consider, though, is your reflection in a mirror a lie? Only if you thought it was real, independent of yourself, and something to build your life around. In other words, only if there was first a misunderstanding are we dealing with lies. *With* understanding, which you can and are obtaining, you see the illusions for what they are—reflections of your thoughts, beliefs, and expectations—and excitingly, instead of this spoiling the adventure, it takes it to a higher place! One of controlled manifestations and thoughtful introspection. The adventure suddenly becomes multidimensional.

Can you almost imagine Divine Intelligence mulling over the possibility of creating time and space, thinking out loud, "Yeah . . . but will 'anyone' (me, myself, and I) ever really believe the illusions are real? Won't such trickery be obvious? Will time, space, and matter seem remotely relevant?" In the exact same way, someone who's never seen a television soap opera might wonder if potential viewers could possibly care, believe in, or be somehow emotionally affected by all the blatantly fake drama . . .

Hell to the YES! Those viewers, as they perhaps watch from their kitchens, knowing that every second they witness is scripted and understanding that the characters are being played by people who live utterly different lives than those they portray, are still swept away with emotion, taking sides, crying poignantly, laughing hysterically, looking on lustfully, as if it were absolutely real; as if they were involved; as if it were their own life! Just like you, here and now. This is your life, but you are so much more. And what you're beginning to realize is that you are not only starring in the lead role, but you are the scriptwriter.

Yes, soap operas are just like a life in time and space—fake, yet gripping! Even when you begin to know all that has been shared thus far in these pages, and you know that life's all illusion, and you know you are an eternal spiritual being, daily you'll still be rocked by your emotions. *Less than before*, but still to a passionate, meaningful degree. And so, suddenly, both soap operas and life on earth become real. Not as realities, but as teachers and for where they can take your heart.

Life in the illusions is like a philosophical isometric exercise in which there are no real moving parts, no one goes anywhere, and everyone contributes their individual and collective thoughts to a grand holographic production for Divine Mind to assimilate, projected upon the unchanging silver screen of space-time.

Popcorn, please. Things are about to get really, really good!

CHAPTER 4

LIVING DELIBERATELY AND CREATING CONSCIOUSLY

Where do beliefs fit in?

How does this work for making money?

Emotions?

Finding romance?

LOVE

Intuition?

When does the Universe take over?

Are we being tested?

Are there processes?

Big picture, what can I do to bring on transformation?

What are we supposed to be learning?

Make this practical for me.

$(\omega \uparrow) \cdot \alpha \dot{\omega} \; \circ r \left(5 - \frac{\omega}{7} \right)$

What about our thoughts that never become things?

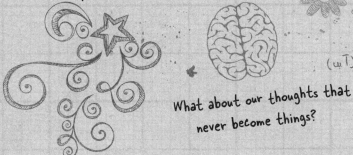

61

Religion was so much easier—good versus evil, God deciding everything, putting the needs of others before my own . . . swaddled in everlasting guilt . . . praying in question marks . . . Well, OK, so religion wasn't all that easy. Instead, you say, I'm loved? A God-Particle? Supernatural? Indestructible? Able to shape my future? I can start happening to life instead of the other way around?

What do I have to do? What does life want from me?

Welcome home! Time to get reacquainted with your hip old stomping grounds, life on earth. It's time for a little refresher on living deliberately and creating consciously upon your floating oasis, amid a loving Universe with supportive principles and conspiring elements.

First, although you may find this rather obvious, *for the wrong reasons*, life is *not* fair. *Hallelujah!* The cards are so stacked in your favor, every second of every day, it's like you're cheating. Remember "Nothing makes you less; everything makes you more"? Now consider, too, that "nothing" and "everything" are never just randomly tossed your way; instead, you only create them when you're ready. Life is not about "how you take it." Sure, you want to roll with the drama until you finally realize you're creating it, but in the grand scheme of things, there's no taking, just making. So, not only are you being added to by every moment of your life, but you get to choose those moments from an infinite palette of possibilities. *Sh-e-e-e-e-ez!*

And it gets better, way better. Your innate, supernatural default setting is to thrive! You are pegged to succeed! *Inclined* to do so within every lifetime (although, in each lifetime, success is entirely up to you) and *destined* to do so overall.

Do you believe it? Or do you see evidence the world over that begs to differ? Stop looking at the world over! *Look at your life for the proof you seek!* Haven't you seen that you are fantastically more inclined to succeed than fail? To smile than frown? To be healthy than ill? To have clarity than confusion? To laugh than cry? Even to have abundance than lack?! It's as if your positive thoughts are 10,000 times more powerful than your negative thoughts, because they are in alignment with the truth of your heritage, being of God, by God, for God, here to rock and roll. Thoughts to the contrary are lies and are, therefore, much harder to manifest than thoughts and statements of truth because they contradict all that makes your very life, this moment, possible.

Life is not fair. Hallelujah!

Life didn't choose you. You chose life. Remember, you came first! Contrary to popular and religious lines of thought, life's presumptive question is not, "What does life want from me?" but *"What do I want from life?"* Your answers will evolve over time. There's never just one, nor are there any wrong answers. Yet each time you answer, adventures will unfold and be made possible, enhanced, and accelerated when you proactively go out and get what you want! The world is your oyster and you are its farmer—a truly symbiotic relationship. This is what you were built to do. The earth exists to make this possible for you and all of its inhabitants.

Make this practical for me.

In spite of the fact that it's generally the outer, physical world you wish to change, the trick is learning that to do so, you must begin within.

If you woke up in the morning and went to the bathroom sink to shave (or to put on makeup), would you apply the shaving cream to your reflection in the mirror? Would you put eyeliner on the glass in front of you? Of course not. Why? Because that's *just a reflection.* Instead, you'd go to the source of the reflection to initiate change, which would then appear in the reflection.

In the physical yet illusionary world, it's the same. You don't have to figure out all the logistics nor manage or manipulate the physical props on your stage and decide upon the perfect marketing and finance plans—although it seems as if you do. You don't have to know the right people at the right time to get the right gig—although it now seems so true. These are all the reflections of the world you've earlier created in your mind through your thoughts, beliefs, and expectations.

Creating change boils down to *what* you know. Particularly in the spiritual, metaphysical sense. If you want to change your fortunes, improve your health, or have creative, fulfilling work, go within. See it in thought. Playfully, as if you were dealing with a make-believe world (which, ahem, it is), visualize that you're already there. These mental images, your thoughts, create molds that the elements of time, space, and matter can rush to fill and that you will meet, as long as you subsequently, physically go out into the world *where you will then* be predisposed to life's so-called coincidences, happy accidents, and serendipities. Without attachment or insistence, thoughtfully and playfully, you might:

1. Dabble with logistics—make some phone calls, call some meetings, put pen to paper, draw schematics, read a book, take a class, or get your license.

2. Consider, study, review possible partners, marketing strategies, financing solutions, and all other known, relevant issues that may contribute to your success.

3. Actually do what you can, with what you have, from where you are, however seemingly inadequate.

Knowing metaphysical truths is no excuse for not getting out more, knocking on doors, and turning over stones; although such knowledge will radically cast your "baby steps" in a brand-new light—making them more fun, easier, less crucial, and more effective.

By first going within, you program and summon life's magic. You do not program the "hows" of your dream coming true; your vision ordains Divine Intelligence to do this for you. You just settle upon and get clear on the *outcome* you seek, your desired end results. In the instant you do this, Divine Intelligence knows all the possible "hows," just like once you give your GPS navigator your desired destination, in a heartbeat, it knows "how" to get you there. Yet the "hows" of your dreams coming true are constantly changing and shifting as you grow and evolve, plus they change and shift as seven billion other players in the world also grow and evolve. Still, at any given moment in time, the shortest, quickest, easiest, and happiest path is known for you to experience the manifestation of your greatest desires, and necessary reroutes are executed on the fly.

The "hows" might be called cursed, given how much you tend to insist upon them. In doing so, not only will you feel you're carrying the weight of the world on your shoulders, since you've effectively excluded all other possibilities, but you'll have limited the ways life's magic can reach you.

In reality, with the "hows" constantly changing because you're constantly changing, as is everyone else, you simply *can't* attach to or insist upon how (nor with whom nor when) your dream will come true, even as *you can* insist upon a totally rocking life of your dreams, which will come with its own hows, whos, and whens, in alignment with all of your other thoughts and dreams.

By physically moving (aka *living your life, out in the world, just doing stuff*), which is metaphorically putting your GPS-led car in gear and driving, you are creating possibilities and so-called miracles through which your life can change, based upon your new thoughts, aka new end results.

THE MIRACULOUS MECHANICS OF MANIFESTATION (YOUR PERSONAL GPS NAVIGATOR):

1. *Give the "system" your desired destination, aka your end result (your hoped-for outcome).* It knows where you are; you just need to tell it where you want to go, and it will work backward, calculating all possible roads you might travel, their speed limits, and traffic—in other words, the "hows"—selecting the route that will take you there the quickest and happiest way.

2. *Take action, show up, go out into the world.* Put your car in gear because the system is designed to *not* help you if your car isn't in gear! Right? Not even a vision board in the backseat will help you. If your car, or life, is in Park, you're beyond help because there's a major contradiction afoot: you have a destination, toward which you refuse to move!

3. *Know that the miracles of our progress are almost always invisible, which doesn't mean they aren't happening!* Do not judge your progress with your physical senses alone, as they were not designed to see the workings of life's magic. Which means you have to go on faith, which can be instilled when you truly understand how the system works, knowing that you're alive in a safe and loving world.

These are the general steps necessary for *all* manifestations, tangible and intangible, for homes or hugs. Curiously, did you notice any hint of Universal or divine judgment—deciding who gets what, when, and where—involved? You did not. Any hint of tests that must be passed? Lessons that must be learned? Sacrifices that must be made? Dues that must be paid? You did not.

All this works, of course, because of the immutable law we spoke of earlier, for which there are no mitigating factors. Your thoughts become things, or better, they become the things *and events* of your life.

What about the thoughts that haven't?

The reason some of the things you've thought about in the past haven't yet come to pass is because other thoughts you've thought about have. The only thing that can block a thought from becoming a thing is *another thought*. Therefore, thoughts in contradiction of stated desires or passionate fears, whether intentionally or accidentally, can keep others from coming to pass. "Can" instead of absolutely "will," because just as you may have unknown contradictory thoughts, so will you very likely have unknown supportive thoughts that may be strong enough to bring the stated desires or fears into being.

Take, for instance, the person who dreams of climbing to the top of the corporate ladder. They want it with their heart and soul. They want it for all of the "right" reasons, to give their family a better life. So, they think thoughts about being in that corner office. They see themselves in their mind's eye, making big decisions, marshaling the forces. Yet if that same person comes home from work every day and says, "Honey, no one at work has any idea of the difference I could make. Honey, nobody at work has any idea of all that I have to offer," those kinds of thoughts must do what all thoughts do: strive and struggle to become part of the thinker's life. And so, the person who thinks they're underappreciated *becomes underappreciated*. And that's not where you want to be if you also see yourself climbing to the top of the corporate ladder.

Just because you don't always get what you most want, doesn't mean you don't always get what you think about. The reason that some of your thoughts have not yet become things is always because other thoughts of yours have, and they got in the way.

Lest you now feel that you are vulnerable to every stray, errant, negative, or fearful thought, worry not. Remember, you are inclined to succeed! You're an ancient, intergalactic gladiator of love and joy, here to creatively set your life ablaze. Remember, your positive thoughts are far more powerful than your negative ones. Therefore, when feeling scared, lonely, lost, confused, angry, hateful, negative, or afraid, simply do your best to understand and banish them, and moreover, don't worry that you worry! You're not vulnerable. You're going to continue rocking your life, just as you have up until now—no matter how else things may appear.

What about the thoughts I didn't think that happened anyway?

Whenever you want more of something in your life, like wealth and abundance, friends and laughter, or less of something, like calories or credit card debt, by working with your thoughts you're actually commissioning the entire Universe to bring about a change. If you will, you're starting this journey from point A in time and space, and you want to move to point B, in time and space. Very often, the only way to make this kind of journey is for your thoughts of point B to draw you through *unthought-of* territory, once your "car is in gear."

This doesn't imply that *anything* could happen in your journey. Everything that does happen in all of your journeys is always predicated and based upon all of your *other thoughts* about life, people, happiness, et cetera. Nevertheless, if you want to effect a change in your life, you're commissioning the Universe to take you on a journey from point A, your starting point, to point B, the place you are *thinking* of, during which you'll be drawn through lots of unthought-of territory.

God doesn't give anything to anyone!
You're here to learn how to give things to yourself.

Metaphorically, when you get in a car to drive for hours, maybe headed to a new friend's home, during your journey you have no idea what smiling or frowning faces you're going to see on the turnpike or in the toll plaza. You have no idea where you're going to stop for gas, where you might stop to rest or get a quick bite to eat. You don't know before that journey begins where the highway might be under construction and force you to take a detour. Yet all of those experiences in your journey will be necessary to get you to your friend's, *the place that you were thinking about.*

The same is true in life. Whenever the unexpected lands on your path, whenever you experience the unthought-of—good, bad or otherwise—it is *always* a stepping-stone in a journey to another place beyond it that you *have* been thinking about.

Wait, earlier you implied there are no tests? I thought life was made up of tests, if not to be judged, then to prepare us for whatever comes next.

Why would you be tested? What would that achieve? *As if* you might be left behind? *As if* you might get moved to the top or bottom of a class that teaches there are no real "tops" or "bottoms"? *As if* Divine Intelligence didn't already know all? *As if* you weren't a love being, motivated by good? *As if* whatever came next for a God-Particle required something that you don't yet have? You're not here to get ready for somewhere else, you are here to be here!

You aren't tested. Never have been. It's another power-robbing idea, including the seemingly benign notion that "God will never give you more than you can handle." *God doesn't give anything to anyone!* You're here to learn how to give things to yourself. That's the name of the game. Yet when you experience the *unexpected*, you assume it couldn't have come from your own thoughts; it must, therefore, be a "test," and there goes your power.

What you experience is *always* a function of your inner energies (prevailing thoughts, beliefs, and expectations), which, when confused, bring about chaotic half-manifestations at best. Secondly, it's not as if there's any such thing that you can't handle; *you're indestructible.* For example, the less appreciative you are of yourself, the less you honor yourself, disregarding the truth of your magnificence, the more it will seem the rest of the world takes you for granted, and, thus, the more trying your circumstances will be. Still, you are eternal. No tests are involved. And nothing can take anything away from your true inner brilliance. There's no going around your creative powers—own them, accept responsibility for them, and ultimately you shall be free of all things unpleasant.

So, what about "lessons"? Aren't we here to learn things?

Yes, but only to the degree that they will help you go bigger, run faster, and live longer, and only if you care to. There are no lessons that you "have to" learn, but many that you want to learn, with as much desire and passion as you might now want a fancy new car or a dream home—even more so. Why? To experience the ecstasy of living deliberately, loving consciously, and knowing all is supremely well! The more you learn, appropriate to the life and experiences you wish to have, whether of patience, love, or other obvious virtues, the more powerful and intentional a creator you become. These lessons, faster than anything else, however seemingly mundane in and of themselves, will get you your fancy new car, dream home, warm hugs, and so much more, including deeper experiences in love, health, and happiness.

Moreover, it's not as if your life, parents, place of birth, and the other givens of your life are random and you just hope to have the opportunity to learn what you most want to learn in your next life. Everyone, always, chooses all the parameters of each lifetime, in large part for the great probability of mastering the lessons they wish to learn. Sweet. Life, your life, was a "setup"! Set up by you! It matters not that today you might not be able to see the reasons for other people's choices, nor recall even your own, particularly among challenging times. You can, nevertheless, rest assured their and your objectives are being met, such is the perfection of this rigged game.

Backing up a bit, I thought it was our beliefs that must first change, not our thoughts? Shouldn't you be saying that our "beliefs become things"?

Your beliefs *are* almighty, not because they override your thoughts, but because they allow you to think, or prevent you from thinking, along certain lines in the first place. In other words, your beliefs are pivotal in all of your creations *because your thoughts become things*, and your beliefs regulate what you can and will think.

Your beliefs *interpret* what you see with your own, unknown prejudices, which in turn *determines how you'll react to what you see*—in thought, word, and behavior. They're like sunglasses, to use them as a metaphor again, in that they filter all your experience. You can sometimes forget you even have them "on." Unlike sunglasses, however, you usually can't just take them off, and that means, generally, *you have no idea of how else life could look, other than how you now see it.* I mean, "Is that the most gorgeous sunrise you've ever seen . . . or am I wearing my blue-blockers again?"

---

*You don't have to know what your invisible
limiting beliefs are to move past them.*

Obviously, then, some beliefs will serve you, while others can hold you back. This leads many on a wild-goose chase after the invisible, limiting, self-sabotaging beliefs they assume they must have. But just because you haven't made the progress you've dreamed of, that does not necessarily mean it was because of your beliefs. Maybe it was priorities? Maybe it was not taking sufficient action? Maybe there's been no problem, and your hoped-for manifestation lies only days away? Yet the person who now believes they have limiting beliefs, even when they don't, ironically runs the risk of creating them through this belief! You needn't go there.

NEW BELIEF ALIGNMENT AND INSTALLATION

A work-around that's much simpler and less dangerous involves these two steps:

1. Name as many beliefs as you can that would support you and your dreams, and then

2. behave, in some small way, daily if possible, as if those beliefs were actually yours.

It's much easier and wiser to name beliefs *you want*, some of which may actually already be yours, than to claim beliefs *you don't want*—some of which probably weren't yours (yet in claiming, they become so).

This approach to installing new beliefs works *even if there are* contradictory, opposing beliefs held by the practitioner. Even if they don't know they have such limiting beliefs. You don't have to know what your invisible limiting beliefs are to move past them. As you name the beliefs you wish were actually yours, and behave as if they were, your new, empowered life begins to emerge for which the old, invisible, unknown beliefs no longer make any sense, to such a degree they fall away into oblivion.

What about our emotions and intuition? These are thoughts too, right? Do they come first, last, or in the middle of the process of creation?

Your emotions, ranging from happy to sad, are your reaction to what's happening on the stage of your life. They come after the manifestation. Whereas feelings, like your intuition and hunches, are more instinctual, at times even bypassing immediate circumstances, to inform or confirm what's happening, or about to happen, in the world with relevance to you. They arrive before and/or during the manifestation.

YOUR EMOTIONS

Your emotional reaction to what's happening in the world provides great insight into your beliefs, and when this matters most is when your emotions aren't fun. This means, *once poked*, your invisible, limiting beliefs aren't so invisible after all. This is not an attempt to go looking for invisible, limiting beliefs, but when you find you're suffering from any unpleasant emotion, it does mean that through choosing to react differently, choosing to see with your inner eyes and from a higher perspective, you can alleviate, for example, the sadness that stems from a broken heart.

Through rightly seeing that you are more than any relationship can define, and that there are indeed countless more opportunities for romance and adventure awaiting once you turn the page.

By tuning in to your emotions, you can immediately know exactly where your illusions have become their most captivating, and misleading, in order to know where best to bring about change and relief.

YOUR INTUITION

The hunch, the gut feeling, the spontaneous sense of knowingness: these are literally "gifts from heaven." Sometimes they seem to arrive on their own; other times you may intentionally summon them. These gifts represent your invisible link to everywhere, always, at once, a link that's never been broken.

They're the sixth sense you've been taught *not* to trust. Yet that hasn't stopped them from raising the hair on your neck, giving you goose bumps, or telling you when you're in the presence of an ancient friend, who in the instant you meet makes you feel deeply understood. Believed in or not, your sixth sense rarely takes a day off from reaching you with warm and witty, cold and scary, or fast and furious insights.

If you'd like to exponentially enrich your journey, it's time to learn the language of intuition—through practice. Go within. Find the quiet. Ask questions. *Feel their answers.* Demonstrate.

When does the loving, "conspiring" Universe enter the picture to show us the way and make our day?

Firstly, "the Universe," of course, is a widely accepted metaphor for a spiritual, nonreligious God. Pretty cool. After all, religion needs spirituality, spirituality does not need religion. "The Universe" is seen as a no-strings-attached, loving essence who dotes on and approves of all "Its" children. Not only does this Universe seemingly refrain from any and all forms of negative judgment, but believers imagine it works feverishly on everyone's behalf—calculating, scheming, aligning, even dreaming for you exactly what you have been dreaming of for yourself. So tireless is She, and patient are believers, that when disappointed with life, they react with, "the Universe has 'Her' own schedule" or "the Universe must have something even better in store for me."

Nice. Warm and fuzzy. Compassionate and forgiving. Loving and supportive. This "She" is certainly closer to truth than an irritable, impatient, jealous "He"! Yet, for the intuitive and logical life explorer, upon closer examination, even this new image appears to be slightly "off."

For instance, consider these implications:

- Isn't any kind of judgment, negative or positive, limiting and exclusive?

- What's wrong with humanity that you are so ineffective without "Her"?

- If "She's" out there watching, who or what are you— entertainment?

- Where was "She" that time you ran into the tree?

Unless, perhaps, "She" is almost none of the things just ascribed to her . . . righto!

So, now what?! There's no angry God and no bubbly Universe?

This is when things start feeling scary again. When you start getting that the truth means:

- You really are special, as special as everyone else.
  Ack! In other words, you're not favored at all!

- The Universe can't and won't live your life for you.
  Uh-oh! In other words, you may as well be alone!

- Everyone has an equal chance at getting whatever they, or you, want.
  Dilution. In other words, there goes your supernatural advantage!

Crushing! Devastating! Rip-off!

Fortunately, getting back to the previous implications, but now viewed through a lens of truth, *drumroll, please . . .*

- *While the Universe is nonjudgmental, this doesn't mean it's neutral.*

- *Thriving is in your nature state; positive thoughts are more powerful than negative ones.*

- *Among illusions, there's more than enough for everyone.*

- *Given your eternal nature, success is assured.*

- *You don't need "Her," you are "Her."*

So, *for none of the reasons ever given before,* like an old-school *God* answering your prayers or a "new-school" Universe favoring you, you'll nevertheless succeed at having, doing, and being all those things you now dream of having, doing, and being—or better. The "or better" being a catchall not just because there *is* better out there than you even knew to ask for, but because sometimes not getting what you now want is better than getting it, *if this is in accordance with all of your other desires!* So, even not getting what you want, in such cases, and with hindsight, is actually getting what you *really* want! You just didn't know, at the time, that you wanted it that way—that you wanted to be blocked until you got your thinking straight, to ensure you could ultimately, irrevocably, *and permanently* move onward and upward.

Every cell and atom in your body is divine and alive, you are divine and alive, upon a planet that is divine and alive.

75

However loopy this sounds and *is*, it's part of the built-in magic that ensures no one will ever get stuck in mediocrity or stagnation. And far from implying you'll always be at the mercy of receiving things you didn't know you wanted, these *exceptions* will soon fade from your experience altogether as you become wiser and happier in your upward spiral.

And so we can say, however new age-y, though not literal, it's far truer than false: the Universe is your greatest conspirator. It roots for you, cheers for you, and loves you throughout every step of your life. It yearns for your happiness and fulfillment, and without a doubt, the cards of life are stacked in your favor because of it. No, it can't and won't reach over your shoulder and manipulate the deck independently of your thoughts and beliefs; to do so would violate your freedom, steal your power, and undermine your responsibilities—negating the very reasons you, and "She," chose to be you in this time and space. But as the Universe yourself, as one of the original fearless explorers who created the jungles of time and space, all of the elements are there for your intents and your purposes. You put them there, and chief among your aims was to thrive in your life on earth.

If all of this were true, wouldn't I be rich by now?

You *are* rich right now! See it. Every cell and atom in your body is divine and alive, you are divine and alive, upon a planet that is divine and alive. Lack, illness, and discord aren't normal for anyone; they're simply the temporary by-products of limited, fearful, and/or contradictory thinking, unless chosen at birth, in which case the gifts they bear are far less obvious and more complicated.

The earth is teeming with countless creatures that live in harmony above, below, and around it. Bursting with intelligent life: an animal kingdom, plant kingdom, and adventurers like yourself. It's lush with abundance and loaded with diversity, filled with dazzling colors, sights, textures, and sounds; with tantalizing sceneries from the plains to the mountains, from the seashores to ocean floors, from valleys to glaciers and deserts; with breathtaking sunrises and sunsets, snowfalls, rains, towering clouds, and crystal-clear blue skies. What's going on here is the blossoming of Divinity, not the decline of planets and species, where every moment and all it contains is born of a super-loving, ever-growing intelligence that connects and celebrates all.

Are you beginning to see how you fit into the equation of reality creation? As a creator yourself? As Divine and sacred, the center of all you experience? Before whom all the elements bow? Born to explore and destined to succeed? Supernatural? Here to inherit the Kingdom? The prodigal child who's lost your way, as all have by design, yet now in the process of ascending into the light to behold the truth of your magnificence and eternal nature?

See this!

How does all this work in relationships? Are soul mates part of the equation?

It all works fabulously in relationships, as long as you're not insisting upon or attaching to *specific* behavior that you want to experience from *specific* people—which would boil down to manipulation. Would you like to live in a world where others could force your behavior or affection based on their thoughts, beliefs, and expectations? Instead, create the space for your dream partner to enter your life, describe them in your mind, imagine the fun and laughter, the travel and surprises, and all that you value. Make yourself available, take some baby steps, but then let the right person show up at the right time! When you insist upon a certain someone, you exclude all other candidates.

If you already have a partner but wish the relationship would go deeper and be more mutually appreciated, then imagine a deeper, more mutually appreciated relationship, but do not insist it must be with your present partner. This, incidentally, does not exclude them from contention. It just means they need to step up to the plate, or else. And it means you've sent out a new vibe to the conspiring Universe that you've raised the bar and it's time to "tango."

The notion of a soul mate being yours by destiny, necessary to complete you, is usually a misguided, romantic attempt to reconcile the dichotomies of living in the illusions. The notion being, if you're a male in this lifetime, you must be balanced by a particular female, and vice versa, and in either case, there's someone "out there" so perfect for you it's as if "God" had arranged it, and all other suitors pale in comparison. The truth is, over all of your lifetimes, you are both male and female, with varying sexual orientations, and in any particular lifetime, you have both male and female energies. What defines you physically does not limit you spiritually. You are complete and whole as is, in spite of your physical gender, which is not to say that your journey, at times, or maybe throughout a lifetime, can't or won't be enhanced with other people in it—defined as partners, family, friends, and the like. But this is never true to the degree that you're incomplete without them.

And while there no doubt exists, at certain intervals in most lives, one single person who better matches you than any of the other seven billion people alive, and with whom you'd be happier and learning more than if you were alone, that person may well change throughout the years! Defining them this way, you would very likely have multiple soul mates in one lifetime—some you would outgrow, others would outgrow you, and, at times, you might have more fun and learning without a partner.

Seems like a lot to know?!

Fear not. Consider that those who are successful in the world today, whether romantically, financially, or in any other way, are so, most typically, in total ignorance of these spiritual principles and truths. You have space stations, DNA technology, transplanetary communication systems that enable anyone to speak to anyone else, all with your spiritual heads in the sand, either afraid of a nonexistent angry God, or thinking that life is pure, random chance. Shocking! And still you thrive.

Can you even begin to imagine what life on earth will look like when her populations understand their divinity? Life's sacredness? Your Godship? *Unimaginably* different. *Unimaginably spectacular!*

Try, anyway, to imagine your educational, political, social, economic, and health-care systems when everyone understands their interconnectedness and inclination to succeed. Imagine future rock stars, athletes, bankers, doctors, accountants, and attorneys all versed in the subject of their divinity, knowing who and what they are; who and what the Universe is, how stunningly powerful their thoughts are, how their beliefs, emotions, and intuitions can be harnessed for direction, and knowing how to deliberately engage life's logistical principles to profoundly change their own journeys and to help other people with theirs. Imagine the joy and love and peace on earth. Mind-blowing, huh? Because it's so different from today, it's even difficult to clearly see. But that's OK.

CHAPTER 5

How to Go Bigger, Run Faster, and Live Longer

What's the most effective way to visualize?

Why is this all making so much sense?

Why do I know so many BIG dreamers who have nothing to show for it?

If thoughts become things, what, if any, action must take on our dreams?

How about angel help?

How can I program my "GPS" and "put my car in gear"?

Destiny?

Miracles?

Fate?

Luck?

What if I can't stop worrying about something?

How do I "take action" but not worry about the "Cursed hows"?

Can we count on these?

I want to know why this all makes so much sense. I want to believe this. I want to get on board.

You're already on board, so is everyone else, it's in your spiritual DNA, it's part of who you are. It's just that you've all been fed contradictory, false ideas like "life is hard, people are mean, and God is angry," to the point you're doubting what you knew to be true. Fortunately, no one can ever completely lose that feeling that only the truth offers, any more than they can lose their eye color. Brushing into truth is like brushing into a long-forgotten friend. It's like a warm philosophical embrace, cozy and reassuring, of something distantly familiar. Only the greatest of fears or the most stubborn arrogance can distance you from it, and then only temporarily. For example, your whole life you've heard people say, "Be careful of what you wish for because you just might get it." And even as you would tell anyone listening that "you can't just make wishes and expect them to come true," you still sense this old adage speaks of a forgotten power. Indeed.

You've also heard about and unquestioningly believe in the powers of positive thinking and the art of creative visualization—the world's top athletes use both.

These platitudes resonate with you and everyone else, regardless of nationality or culture, because you have the innate ability to sense the truth about all things in life, even before it has words, long before tests prove it to be. The truth exists, is absolute, benign, friendly, and, above all, knowable. Instinctively *you know* that you're powerful, worthy, and deserving of all that your heart desires. Instinctively, you know that you're a divine, magnificent, spiritual being for whom all things are possible. And instinctively, deep down, you sense that all of these clichés have meaning, because deep down you also sense, and have witnessed, *your thoughts become things*.

Thoughts become things. Not sometimes but all the time. Not just your positive thoughts, but the other ones too. It's an immutable law as rigid, as predictable, and every bit as dependable as gravity. In fact, no one can *ever* turn it off.

But this isn't bad news! It's awesome news because they're *your* thoughts, and every minute of every day you get to choose exactly what you're going to think. And with this principle, you can bring virtually anything you can imagine into your life, and it's not just limited to material things. You can imagine more love, more joy, and more laughter.

How do we do this? How do our thoughts become things?

When you dream at night about people, places, or circumstances, are those people, places, and circumstances real or are they just thought? Yeah, tricky, because for the person having the dream, perhaps with sweaty brow, racing heart, and other bodily functions reacting taking place, the people, places, and circumstances of the dream *are real*. Yet to the friendly observer, who's maybe watching you toss and turn through the dream, those people, places, and circumstances are just your imagination, pure thought.

With the Big Bang, "God's" thoughts
became the entire Universe, yet . . .
look who's thinking now, kiddo.

The answer is "both." The people, places, and circumstances of any nighttime dream are real *and* thought. Why would being one preclude it being the other? Haven't scientists proven matter isn't solid, but whirling, organized energy? Why would you think that for something to be real, it must be tangible? Or why would you think that thoughts are *"just your imagination,"* as if that meant they weren't real? Scientists have also shown that thoughts possess energy to a detectible degree, and they will soon be proving much, much more.

Parallel insights can be drawn from the dream called *"here and now."* Except, if you will, somewhat metaphorically (and somewhat literally), this dream was dreamt by "God" . . . who is now, slowly but surely, waking up mid-dream, sleepy, confused, groggy . . . *within* humanity, within the dream, as each man, woman, and child who has ever lived, is now living, and will ever live. Again, the baton has been passed. You, God-Particle that you are, now perpetuate this dream. God is still holding it together, on autopilot, as it were, but as you awaken, you find that not only do you get to choose your thoughts, but they can easily be seen to influence what happens next in your life on earth. Thus, your choices today are feeding the waking dream of your life—as they always have but without you being aware.

With the Big Bang, "God's" *thoughts became the entire Universe*, yet . . . look who's thinking now, kiddo. You, individually and collectively, are literally streaming matter into space. Wherever you focus your attention and therefore energy, worlds are born. *Just like in a nighttime dream.*

At a global level, the population's thoughts create mass events. The stock market rising or falling, real estate prices going up or down. These occurrences are either direct thoughts and fears or indirect thoughts and fears, on a collective scale, that lead to shared manifestations. So, just as an individual creates his or her own life by the thoughts they think, so does a family, a neighborhood, a city, a country, or a civilization create its own environment. We talked about this earlier in terms of the weather.

But this seems grossly oversimplified. As if the starting point for everyone was the same. It's not. It's never the same. People are wildly different. There can't be a one-size-fits-all answer to who gets what, why, and when.

But there can be, there must be an answer that fits all, otherwise nothing would ever reconcile. Your premise needs reexamining; you're coming from the old-school *everybody-gets-one-life-to-live* perspective? Right? This sneaks in. Back up, reset, go forward. To compensate for varying experiences due to the various parameters of a life that you mentioned, you come back again and again until you've worn all the hats you've chosen to wear. While here, however, the rules apply the same to all: thoughts become things. The variable is YOU and what you choose to think, not the principle that forges matter.

The differences in people, their behavior, their successes and failures, boil down to what they think. The single commonality between people with similar experiences is always and only their thoughts. For example, what makes people fabulously rich? Are they all white? All Christian? All tall? Short? Skinny? Heavy? From the Far East, Near East, or West? Are they all saintly Goody Two-Shoes? Are they all crooks? Did they all get master's degrees in business schools? Are they all good-looking or otherwise-looking? What? What? What? *Ask!!*

The variable is YOU and what you choose to think,
not the principle that forges matter.

The answer exists, as knowable and recognizable as the Rolls-Royces they may drive. *BUT-YOU-MUST-ASK!*

Ah . . . ! Do they all have high IQs or EQs? That's a BIG N.O.— just look at the people with mountains of money! Rarely are they the "sharpest tools in the shed."

So, what then? What one thing do they all have in common . . . besides cash?

They all believed that it could happen to them. They all dreamed and imagined either avalanches of cash crashing into their lives or of something else happening, unrelated to cash, yet that would consequently, intentionally or unintentionally, create avalanches of cash. And once you believe something, you can't help it, it's the nature of "things," you automatically start *thinking more and more thoughts* along the lines of your beliefs, which ultimately means you start dreaming, imagining, speaking, and behaving along those lines. And once you go there, what happens next? Your thoughts *will become* the things and events of your life—*it's the law.*

And what of fate? Destiny? Angel help? Miracles? Luck? The right people at the right time? Second chances? Gray areas or wiggle room?

Second chances, helping angels, miracles, luck, meeting the right people at the right time, are all ordained by your thoughts and the "absolute law" that brings them to life, not the other way around! It's what creates your fate and destiny, which can change as often as you change your mind. *Thoughts become things.*

To see this in its simplest form, what happens when someone throws a ball into the air? *Right!* Midway through its journey, it begins falling back down to earth. Why? *Because it has to. It's the law.* Now, let's make this a little more complicated, so that you really get how simple it is.

In order for that ball to begin falling back down to earth:

- Does it matter *who* threw it?

- Does it matter how old they think they are or how young they really are?

- Does it matter how good-looking and popular they are?

- Does it even matter whether or not *they know about gravity and the principles of physics* for that ball to come back down to earth?

No! Nothing matters once they throw that ball, because as it leaves their fingertips, the Universe and its principles take over. *And that's exactly what happens once you choose your thoughts. So, choose them . . . wisely.*

Let's just say, hypothetically, if someone was coming around to this way of thinking . . . what might you suggest they do to harness this power? How would they program their "GPS," as you put it, and "put their car in gear"?

First be sure you, *they,* understand that anyone really only has three points of contact with life's magic or this principle: their thoughts, their words, and their actions. Not to make this complicated. Everything still boils down to *thoughts becoming things,* but you speak your thoughts as well. Your words are nothing more than your thoughts charged with enough urgency that they roll off of your tongue. Your actions are nothing more than your thoughts charged with so much intention that they've thrown you into motion. Which tips us off as to how and where you can begin deliberately using this principle of *thoughts becoming things* to spark major life changes.

> *You only need to do what you can, with what you have, from where you are, and it will be enough to turn any tide in your favor.*

Let's look at these three points of contact from two angles, defensively and offensively. Defensively, you'll want to become aware of everything you think, say, and do, to minimize patterns that aren't in alignment with your dreams and desires. Offensively, you'll look for ways of inciting change and demonstrating intention, deliberately sparking new thoughts, words, and behaviors so that you can install new beliefs, create a heightened state of expectation for success, and manifest new patterns of experience that start serving you.

USING YOUR THOUGHTS

Obviously, if your thoughts are what shape your future, wouldn't it be ideal to consider what you've been thinking lately? Versus what you could be thinking? Which is easier than you might think.

Defensively

Simply monitor yourself. Be an observer. Become aware of what you're thinking and, to the degree possible, do not allow yourself to continue focusing on things that do not serve you. The more you think about something, the more you either draw it forth or perpetuate its existence in your life. Your thoughts are not just thoughts. They're the building blocks of your tomorrows. When you discover those that are unhelpful, to the best of your ability, change "the channel."

For times when you've got a runaway train of fear tearing through your mind and you just can't stop the negativity, let it go. Allow it to run its course. Again, don't worry that you worry. Remember, you're inclined to succeed and your positive thoughts are far more powerful than your fearful and worrisome thoughts. Then, simultaneously start a new train running. Sit down and visualize. Direct at least some of your thoughts to images that do serve you, even as the fear train runs. This *will* seem utterly futile, but do it anyway. Even as you muster a few happy thoughts, you may find the negativity taking over; do it anyway. Again and again in your past you have prevailed against all odds, and this is why. You only need to do what you can, with what you have, from where you are, and it will be enough to turn any tide in your favor. If you just attempt to do your part, it will *always* be enough. Pretty good odds, huh? *Again, almost as if you were "cheating"!*

Offensively

Visualize. And don't just wait for runaway trains of negative thinking to emerge before you try this out! If you understand that your thoughts become the things and events of your life, how could you not spend just a little bit of time every single day deliberately thinking thoughts of the life of your wildest dreams as if you were already living it? To this end, here are six guidelines that may help. They're not rules. This is all about *thoughts becoming things*. That's the only rule there is. But to help you with your thoughts and to help you make them become things, these guidelines can get you started with a simple, daily practice.

Visualization Guidelines

1. **Just do it once a day.** That's it. One time a day, and then drop it. Get back to the here and now, appreciating who you already are and all you already have. Do not start doing it 27 times a day, thinking that it will be 27 times more effective than if you did it just once. If you visualize 27 times or even 7 times a day, there's a tendency to start comparing where you dream of going to where you are here and now. And if you're spending so much time between the two worlds, you may become overwhelmed with the seemingly great distance you have to travel, become psyched out, demoralized, maybe even give up. Don't risk it! Don't become overwhelmed. And don't start living in the future when your happiness does most certainly spring from the here and now. Solution: one time a day, and you're done until tomorrow.

2. **Don't visualize longer than 5 or 10 minutes.** That's the max, not the ideal. Three or four minutes a day would be awesome. The reason not to visualize longer than 5 or 10 minutes is because no matter who you are, if you try to visualize longer than 5 or 10 minutes, you are going to start daydreaming. And then you're going to get mad at yourself. Then you're going to label yourself adult ADD, and then you're going to draw the conclusion that you can't do it, and it doesn't work for you. Don't go there. In fact, you might use a countdown timer so that you aren't wondering during the exercise how much

time you have left. Once you visualize for 3 or 4 minutes, you've made your mark. You've created the impression of what it is you want. Those thoughts are now striving to become the things and events of your life. Doing it longer than 10 minutes is completely unnecessary and, in fact, may be counterproductive.

3. **Imagine every possible detail**. When you're visualizing, consider and include every conceivable detail. See the sights, hear the sounds, smell the aromas, feel the textures, put in all of these details, and, for extra credit, put in some extraneous details. For instance, imagine you're in the corner office of your brand-new world headquarters. You're sitting at your desk. The phone rings. How does the phone ring in your brand-new world headquarters? Pick up the receiver. How does it feel in your hand? Answer it. Who's on the other end? What are they saying to you? Comment back. Put in these extra details, because while they may have nothing to do with your dream itself, they have everything to do with making the image in your mind more real. Do the same imagining for the furniture in your world headquarters. Take a glance at it. Look at the paintings that are on the wall. Look out the window behind you. What do you see? Are there woods, a pond, a parking lot? All of these extra details make the image in your mind more real. When you're visualizing, clarity is power.

4. **Feel and imagine the joy**. It's just one more detail, but it's such an important detail that it gets its own guideline, and it's the detail of emotion. Emotion acts like a power booster for all manifestations. It makes the whole process happen faster. Emotion is what you're really after, right? The reason you want more money or more friends or improved health is always

for the emotion of joy and happiness. So when you're visualizing, feel the joy, feel the happiness. This is the single most important detail to include when you're visualizing.

5. **Put yourself in the picture**. This is critical but easy to overlook. See yourself in the picture. It needs to be you and your life that's being played out on the "movie screen" of your mind, not just pretty, detached scenery. You want to imply ownership.

   You don't want to just manifest fleeting glimpses of your dream life, you want them to be permanent. You don't want to just be invited for tea to your dream home, you want to be hosting tea in it. You don't want to just be loaned a new, red, sporty Mercedes, you want your name on the title. Put yourself in the picture!

   See yourself in the driver's seat of your dreamed-of car, feel *your* hands on its steering wheel, feel yourself reaching over to program its stereo. Or imagine *your* hand in the palm of someone else's as you walk along the beach one romantic evening. Or imagine *your* toes in the sand.

6. **Always and only dwell upon the end result**. When you're visualizing, always and only dwell upon the desired end result of your dream coming true, or beyond. Never worry about the "hows." How your dreams will come true is beyond your ability to know, yet this doesn't jeopardize that you can still know it will. The logistics for any single day on earth to unfold, as said earlier, with seven billion co-creators who are constantly changing their plans, dreams, and minds, is why you can't say "this" is "how that" will happen without possibly throwing a wrench into the machinery. Yet it's no big deal for Divine Mind. When you *insist* on hows, they become the "cursed

hows," because you're putting all of your eggs in one basket, stressing yourself out, and eliminating from contention innumerable other paths that Divine Mind could have used to make your dream come true. Yes, it might work when you insist upon a "cursed how"—sometimes it has for you in the past—but going forward, is "might" good enough anymore? Let Divine Intelligence do its job, weaving together the paths, desires, and thoughts of everyone alive.

USING YOUR WORDS

Again, your words are nothing more than your thoughts, spoken. When similarly monitored, they can tip you off as to what you're silently and sometimes unknowingly thinking, creating the opportunity to make changes when necessary.

Defensively

Do your best to stop talking poorly of yourself, your friends, your enemies, life, and pretty much anything else you may be bad-mouthing. By choosing to talk about the things, people, and circumstances you don't like, you draw more of the same to you.

This doesn't mean accepting things you don't like. It also doesn't mean you aren't justified in or deserving of your anger, resentment, or whatever you're feeling. And it doesn't mean forever being silent or doing nothing. What it does mean is realizing you always have a choice, and your choices have consequences. It means realizing that to repeatedly—over weeks, months, or years—lament, complain, or moan about unpleasing conditions makes them get worse and last longer!

Offensively

Conversely, when you catch yourself excessively complaining—or if you simply want to reaffirm and interject conditions you'd like to experience—choose empowering words. You can start speaking about your life as if it is already a reflection of your dreams. Or start speaking about yourself as if you are already the person you've always dreamed you'd one day be. It takes so little to offer this spark that can set fires of change raging. Words aren't just words, they're your thoughts that will become things the soonest because of the energy and intention required of you to speak them, over all other choices.

*You always have a choice, and
your choices have consequences.*

You don't need a life coach to choose empowering words. You don't need any more self-improvement books. You don't have to figure out who you were in the 4th century. You just need to start saying things that serve you, whether or not they're even true in the beginning. Say things like, "My life is easy! I love my life! I have absolute clarity with what I'm going to do for the rest of my life! *Total clarity.* I always say exactly the right thing at exactly the right time to the exact right person." How many people say the exact opposite and wonder why they never have the right thing to say at the right time to the right person?

"I am surrounded by wealth and abundance! Everything I touch turns to gold." Remember, say these things even when they're not true. In fact, say them especially when they're not true. This is *exactly* why you're saying them—because you want to change the condition you're speaking of to something different from what you are presently manifesting. And know, as with any exercise, you can't start saying new things and look for instantaneous results. You keep at it, in addition to all else you were or could be doing to incite change, and you give it time. After all, it took time to create the conditions you now live in.

And don't forget to say, "I am so photogenic! I can't take a bad picture. The camera loves me." Because this "stuff" (your thoughts and words becoming things) works with *everything*—photogenic potential, energy levels, health, friendships, confidence, creativity, fulfillment, money . . . everything.

Whatever you're talking about, you're going to be bringing about. So decide in advance on some things to say that will serve you. As often as possible, choose to speak about what's working. What's right. And what you love.

Using Your Actions

Your actions are your thoughts in motion.

Defensively

Start paying attention to your everyday, routine behaviors to understand what your thinking is, and then deliberately work on changing those behaviors that need it most. For example:

Being overly frugal: When in the grocery store, do you often shop for the cheapest, most generic brands, trying to save every single penny you can? What does that reveal about your belief in the avalanches of abundance that are rushing toward you? Not much. To counter this, go on the offense and, every now and then, splurge. You don't have to buy all the expensive stuff, but be aware of your behavior and *occasionally* offset that which was not serving you. And remember, your positive "demonstrations," like small splurges, like your positive thoughts, will be at least 10,000 times more powerful than their more negative counterparts. So it's not like you have to splurge on everything. For 19 out of 20 products, buy the cheapest brand; for the other one, splurge. The tiniest demonstrations are fantastically amplified! This is why and how it takes so little, apart from consistency, to succeed.

Losing weight: When it comes to the types of food you buy, do you usually buy low-fat, low-calorie, diet-this, diet-that? If so, every single purchase is screaming to the Universe, "I have a weight problem!" To which it undoubtedly, silently shouts back: "I know! I 'heard' you the first 7,412 times. I'm on it! Don't worry. I'll put you in the wrong place at the wrong time with the wrong people, dispose you to the wrong foods, and give you low self-esteem and slow metabolism! Roger! Gotcha!" This is the power triggered by your actions. Not just dragging you down and bumming you out, but perpetuating the situation you are believing in or preparing for! So believe in and prepare for, occasionally, within reason, never risking your solvency or sanity, the opposite of what you don't want—what you do want!

You don't have to, nor should you, eat all the fattening foods. Just every now and then indulge, as if you are already the perfect weight, with the perfect figure, happy as a lark. Play both ends to the middle; cut calories *and* occasionally indulge. Act as if you are already the person you now dream of being.

In love: When it comes to romantic relationships, are you guarding your heart? Because it was broken before and you don't want *that* to happen again? When you behave that way, your demonstration of mistrust is actually going to draw the worst possible behavior from the person you're having a relationship with. Instead, every now and then, you owe it to yourself and to them to trust. Raise the bar. They will notice, and you'll maximize the chances that their behavior will please you.

Offensively

On the offense, as you've just read, every now and then go out of your way to act as if you know of the inevitable, imminent arrival of your dream. Or, similarly, act as if your dream has *already* come true and you're now living in a world with its manifestation behind you. Acting "as if" emboldens confidence, heightens positive expectations, and puts you out in the world where there can then be serendipities and so-called accidents and coincidences that were actually orchestrated by your earlier dreams and visions, eventually leading you to a life on earth that will physically mirror what you were originally thinking about, speaking to, and pretending was real.

When you use your thoughts, words, and actions wisely, you literally end up rearranging all the players, circumstances, and props on the stage of your life. You actually begin to design your future from among the most favorably infinite probabilities that will then exist, far beyond your conscious awareness, yet mildly dependent upon your other thoughts and where the world is. All of which will inevitably, wildly exceed your greatest expectations, which are always limited by their inability to consider all that is always truly available to you.

I hate to be a spoiler, but I know too many people who live in their heads, off in the future, claiming to be who they aren't, and their lives never seem to change. Why have they failed?

Often the intoxicating euphoria felt over having discovered truth—realizing that you're not being judged, that you're adored, that all things are possible, that your thoughts become things—leads "initiates" to mistakenly conclude that their unbridled excitement and enthusiasm will be enough to change their lives.

Thinking big but acting small, or being excited but playing it safe, are both the same as thinking small.

It won't. Remember, knowing metaphysical truths is no excuse for not getting out more.

Being excited about the truth is not enough to change your life. You must *live* it. Embody it. You have to be out in the world. Eat, sleep, and breathe it. Let down your guard, go out on a limb, and take a few "chances." Predicate your behavior, all that you think, say, and do, upon the truth and upon your vision for the future. Take those first few steps as the brand-new person you've discovered yourself to be, demonstrating that your old worldview is truly history. Because, after all, thinking big but acting small, or being excited but playing it safe, *are both the same as thinking small.*

Go Fish

Let's say you fish for a living. And let's also say that a genie will tell you tonight in your dreams that the next seven days will be the luckiest seven days of your entire life. Tomorrow morning when it comes time to go fishing, would you go with one pole or many? You'd go with as many poles as you could get your hands on. You'd call up everybody in your extended family: "Come on over! Tomorrow's going to begin the luckiest seven days of my entire life! Let's go fishing!" You wouldn't wake up tomorrow morning, open the front door, look to the sky, and say, "Where's the fish? This is supposed to be my lucky week!"

Even people naïve enough to believe in luck are still wise enough to know that it won't do them any good unless they're out there in the world where it can reach them. It's the same when it comes to your thoughts becoming things. It does you no good if you're not out there in the world, reachable. If you want to maximize your reachability, then do *all* you can with *all* you've got from where you are. Which is not to imply that massive action on your part is mandatory, though it may be helpful. It's not that your efforts will be doing the heavy lifting anyway, they'll simply allow for a connection with life's magic. The magic does the heavy lifting. But because you don't know when the next magical lightning bolt will strike, nor the "shortest, happiest route" for you to take, you will improve your odds of it finding you by being reasonably available. This is simply a call to work smart, a call to understand that the Universe needs you to be out living your life so that there can be those supposed accidents, coincidences, and serendipities.

Isn't it contradictory to say I must take action but I'm never to worry about the "cursed hows"? Isn't taking action a form of worrying about the hows?

The thing that makes a cursed how a cursed how is not *what* you do but how you view the reason you're doing it. After all, as shared earlier, there will one day be an identifiable "how" through which the dream came true. Whether or not the how you are speculating upon, pre-manifestation, however, is cursed, depends on whether or not it's attached to or insisted upon to the exclusion of all other "hows." For example, "This book I'm writing will be endorsed by someone famous, which will help it debut on the *New York Times* bestseller list, selling millions of copies, and I will live happily ever after." Phew! That's a lot of pressure! Some important pieces of this puzzle must fall together perfectly, or it's not going to happen! Moreover, there's no room for an alternative to be envisioned. Definitely write the book and dream that it does well, but do not attach your future well-being to it so tightly. This way you're not ruling out or limiting its chances for success, but neither are you closing the door on a million other ways your life could blast off and thrill you. *The "why" in writing the book should be viewed as creating possibilities, as opposed to creating the one and only path.*

Another way you might taint a "how" as cursed would be to view the mortal steps you're taking as sufficient in and of themselves to make your dream come true, instead of seeing your baby steps as sparks that will enable your higher self, life's magic, or Divine Intelligence to get involved and thereby make your dream come true. Can you imagine the pressure that would come from thinking your little baby steps are responsible for making all of your dreams come true? *Don't slip!* Instead, know that for every little step you take, the Universe takes thousands more on your behalf. The more you take, the more She takes! *This* is why you take baby steps, not for the distance they cover. This is how you would ideally view "why you took them": to stir up life's magic. The magic, which is hardly mysterious, does the heavy lifting, but only when you first do your part, the baby steps.

By taking action for the "wrong" reasons, you demonstrate a misunderstanding of your role in the creation of your life events, which, when combined with the stress they'd cause, would work against your inclination to succeed. For clarity, know that:

- you are the captain, not the engineer, of your life's manifestations, and,

- when your life mingles with others' lives, as it must do on a daily basis around friends, clients, customers, peers, etc., there will be co-pilots in your midst, and you won't be creating alone. Which simply means you cannot insist upon who does what (unless they're your kids or your employees, but even then you must not hinge your happiness on their performances).

You simply can't know, because it's not knowable, either with whom, how, where, or when your dreams will come true. Any declaration to the contrary is futile and risks blocking countless "better hows" from ever reaching you. Instead, know only your desired outcome and never stop doing something, anything, about it. Remain open to any and all things that show up along the way, including detours, seeming setbacks, and fickle friends.

Got it . . . pretty cool . . .

Pretty cool? Really? If you really get this, you truly understood all that's just been shared, and if you were to be given just one wish that would absolutely be granted, I know what you'd wish for. There's only one thing that makes any sense. You'd wish for things to be *exactly* as they now are. To be alive as a conscious creator, deliberately living in a paradise cloaked in the illusion of matter, where going bigger, running faster, and living longer depends entirely upon what you choose to think, say, and do. Life really couldn't be any easier than the way it already is.

CHAPTER 6

←→

UNDERSTANDING ACCIDENTS, SETBACKS, AND DISASTERS

Does anyone ever get permanently lost or stuck here?

Whose thoughts were those?

Why would someone choose to be born into a poor or dangerous country or to have terrible or absent parents?

Does life's magic skip over some people?

Doesn't "God" have thoughts of "Her" own that will become things?

What about natural disasters?

Aren't you effectively blaming the victim of every atrocity and violation?

How do you explain when children are hurt, or worse?

What if my higher self disagrees with the dreams of my mortal self?

Just as it all starts making sense, new questions come to mind, like how to reconcile life's disappointments when the unexpected happens, particularly accidents, setbacks, or disasters. Where do these come from? Seems we aren't so powerful after all.

Asking those questions places you at the same fork in the road civilizations before you arrived at—who then chose to advance into perilous terrain. Ultimately leading to the demise of all they loved, in physical terms. Without putting it into words, they viewed the unexpected as irrefutable evidence that life happens *to* you, that you are impotent before nature, a pawn in life's circumstances, the guinea pig of a sadistic god, or the earlier-mentioned "afterthought." Yet it was through such gaping holes in the tapestry of their life's understandings, whether false conclusions or merely unanswered questions, that their power over the illusions slipped away. And in today's life on earth, where are there any holes larger than the contradiction between you being the absolute creator of your life and the seemingly unpredictable and often devastating consequences of the unexpected?

Ask exactly these kinds of questions, wonder, open your heart to new possibilities, and from within you'll find the simple, absolute truths the entire world now so deeply craves and deserves. *All* questions have answers, and that you asked shows those answers are near. This is the height of being spiritually responsible, particularly in a world that encourages you to follow the supposed safety of the herd.

Your quest will ultimately reveal how the very same seemingly mystical mechanics and metaphysical forces that yield the precisely timed "chaos" seen in so-called accidents, setbacks, and disasters, are actually being employed by all alive today, in less than optimal terms, as you individually and collectively create life on earth. This realization is the first step in learning how you can deliberately change your planetary future and individually harness your power to create more abundance, love, and fun—for all.

As you would expect, there's not a sound-bite answer for these questions. Just to review: at the outset, on the path to understanding the unexpected, recall that whenever the "unthought of" lands on your path, it's *always* a stepping-stone in a journey to a farther place that you *have* been thinking about. The reason that sometimes things happen that you never thought about ahead of time is always because just beyond their manifestation lie "destinations" (other pending manifestations) that you *did think about*— whether you desired or feared them. And the only way that the pending "destination" could become a thing was for you to first be drawn through the unexpected. Remember, however, unexpected does not equate to random. Whatever happens will always be within the scope of all your other thoughts about your circumstances and life.

---

*All questions have answers, and that you
asked shows those answers are near.*

This is exactly the case when it comes to "accidents." They're rarely an end in themselves—unless fear, anticipation, and preparation preceded them for no other reason but their potentiality—but a means to accomplish *something else* that was thought of, expected, or believed in *by all affected*. A furtherance of life's journey for the survivors *and* for those who are now on "bigger and better adventures" beyond time and space—all in alignment with the individual and collective thoughts, beliefs, and expectations of everyone involved, about everything that just transpired.

Is that supposed to explain natural disasters? Lunatics running loose with guns? Earlier you said we are the cause of weather patterns, so what about tornadoes, hurricanes, and earthquakes that affect masses of people? It doesn't seem to matter what any of them are thinking, does it? In 2004 a tsunami wiped out over 200,000 unsuspecting men, women, and children on the Pacific Rim and African coasts. How do these catastrophic events make sense?

Of course, seen at "street level," with human eyes and physical senses, that tsunami does appear to be a chance occurrence that brought nothing but horror to an entire region of the world. Yet with spiritual eyes and inner senses, this "tragedy" can be seen very differently.

As we've been discussing, just as an individual's thoughts will craft their immediate environment, so do mass thoughts craft the environment of those sharing it. Therefore, every soul affected by what happened that day in 2004, whether they were washed away, narrowly escaped, or saw it on the news from the comfort of their home, was a participant in and co-creator of what happened, and all chose their vantage point from among options defined by earlier choices (thoughts) that led up to that moment in time. This was a mass event, or call it a mass reflection, caused by mass, cumulative thoughts and tensions that expressed in an agreed upon "now." And where each person would be exactly, geographically, at this time, would be part of each individual's creation/reflection as well.

Why would anyone choose to create such a horrific event?

There are as many different reasons as there were people aware of and affected by what happened. However, to uncover some of their possible rationales, we should first get rid of the "horrific" judgment.

Your limited view of reality, from within time and space, makes it nearly impossible to see anything like this in a positive light. With your physical senses, you think, "Oh my gosh, what good could *possibly* come from a village disappearing in a tidal wave?" But when you realize that death is just the closing of one door so that another can swing open; that those who "perished" are now as aware, individualistic, and "themselves" as they were when "alive"; that the exact time, circumstances, and drama surrounding each individual "death" were handled and calculated with absolute precision in congruence with that person's thinking and logistically "planned" in realms beyond the curtains of time and space, under grace, in divine ways; and that each life only "transitioned" because they were ready, then suddenly it becomes almost absurd to interpret such an event with your physical senses alone. Instead of labeling it "horrific," a sense of order, even perfection, begins to emerge.

When you then consider that *everyone* actually moved on to new adventures that will make them even more magnificent, even love enters the equation.

So, you mean to say that every single death, dismemberment, and crippling, not to mention the loss of loved ones experienced by those who survived, was deliberate? That everyone along the affected coastlines that day was there by their own design? That almost a quarter of a million people drowned because it was "their time" and, coincidentally, they were all within reach of the tide at exactly the right time?

Yes, all of that, except for the "coincidentally" part. While every single person's experience that day was private, and their participation in the event was first and foremost for their own reasons, each was also either willing or intent on being part of this mass event.

There's no such thing as a coincidence. There's no such thing as an accident. You live in a *dream* world. Consider, when you have a dream at night in which you dance with friends, argue with strangers, stub your toe, or find a lion chasing you, would any such occurrence be an accident, random, and meaningless? Or can you sense that any and all such dreams would be part of a creation (however hard to decipher) that reflected certain fears, achieved certain lessons, or revealed certain meaning for the dreamer? It's the same in the "dream" of life. You merely live among illusions of your own creation, having forgotten that you are their creators. Not a single raindrop falls on anyone's head as "an accident." Nor in life do you dance with friends, argue with strangers, stub your toe, or run from fears, randomly or without meaning. Not to imply that there's always some profound, deep meaning beneath every physical occurrence, but some degree of your own thoughts, beliefs, and expectations are always involved, if only thinking, "Crap happens!"—and so it does.

It seems pure lunacy to deny luck, accidents, and mistakes don't happen, when we see they do every single day of our lives, sometimes with heartbreaking, life-or-death consequences. Especially when children or even babies are involved. Why would anyone choose to participate in such an event?

Again, there'd be as many reasons as there were people involved. In some cases, like famine or drought, participation in a mass event might be like a mass protest, locally or globally, against the horrible living conditions under which they exist, no thanks to the rest of humanity, who perhaps did nothing when, in some cases, they could have done much. Or, for example, participants in a genocide might be protesting prevailing ideologies that create war after war, decade after decade. They might be saying "enough is enough" and hitting a Reset button, not just for themselves, but to shock survivors (again, locally and/or globally) into reexamining their lives so that these kinds of things aren't allowed to happen again.

*Not a single raindrop falls on
anyone's head as "an accident."*

As these disasters catch the world's attention, they serve as a wake-up call for those who watch or learn of the suffering on the news, maybe even from 12,500 miles away. If nothing else, seeing families ripped apart, you might hold yours a little bit closer. You might see life in a totally different way. You might treasure its fragility in ways that you had not before the calamity. The calamity, therefore, sparking a new world order.

Meanwhile, each single participant, for their own reasons, found it to be an ideal and perfect drama to be involved in, even if it brought about their "death." This is not to imply that anybody, ever, "deserves" or is to be "blamed" for what happens. Nor does it justify the evil things people have done to those who perished because of them. The concepts of blame, fault, and victimhood that sometimes arise from a "Law of Attraction" worldview—called a "blame the victim" mentality—stem from the old belief that things can randomly happen to anyone. They can't. Words like *blame* and *victim* depend on these misunderstandings. Remove the misunderstandings, and you will find the words don't work anymore in spiritually aware conversations.

Yes, but coincidences? Everyone has them. How can they be timed to such supposed perfection, tying together hundreds of thousands of lives, if not millions or billions? Wouldn't it be more appropriate to acknowledge that people are extremely good at making the best of whatever happens, thereby often turning odd occurrences into pivotal transition points in their lives, rather than denying coincidences?

Oh, yes, agreed, people are truly masters at making the best of whatever happens, maintaining hope when it truly appears lost, but that does not mean that whatever happened was random. You're still trying to explain time-space occurrences with the presumption that life on earth originates, unfolds, and is created on a time line, missing that the time line is secondary. Their end results, those most desired or feared manifestations, dictate the time line. Just because you perceive that things happen in consecutive moments doesn't mean they do. There is another realm invisible to you, in which trillions of probabilities are synthesized into those most believed in by all participants, for every second of every day of your life on earth, which puts everyone in the right place at the right time for their corresponding manifestations. Time is an illusion, right? Therefore, in a greater context, all moments exist at once; it's only your selective awareness that moves and flows linearly. This is *the* hook to living in the jungles of time and space.

To return to the analogy of a Hollywood movie and its production: they don't film movies sequentially, on a linear time line that mirrors the time line portrayed in the film. Sometimes they'll actually film the movie's ending *before* they film the beginning. Usually they film the key pivot-points of the movie first. They edit and clean it all up, see how much time they've used, how much time they have left, see where one event starts and ends, where the next might begin. Later they film filler clips and b-roll so that the important scenes can segue into each other flawlessly, as if they were all "meant to be." Once everything is finished, for the person watching the film on a time line from the comfort of their movie theater seat, it all seems like, "Wow! OMG! What a surprise! Who could have thought of that ending?" Well, they probably thought of the ending before they thought of the beginning, and they perhaps filmed it in that order. What you want to realize from this is, similarly, your life is not the product of "things that happen in time and space"; instead, things happen in time and space *because of you*, just like things happen in a movie because of the writer and the script.

There are no accidents.

Your thoughts, beliefs, and expectations, commingled with those of seven billion other people, force and rearrange the circumstances of your lives to lead you into serendipities and so-called accidents and coincidences, which then set the stage for you to experience the results of what you were originally thinking.

Life is not what it appears to be. The tsunami, therefore, like any event on earth, did not first happen on a linear time line. Instead, it's as if the "desired" effect for every single soul involved was known first, and then all the circumstances and events necessary to produce these were then woven around the probable, not destined, disaster, at which point the earth and the waves rolled.

Incidentally, this is part of the reason why when you visualize something you want to happen, you should start with the *end result* in mind and never mess with the cursed hows—the hows will be forced by the vision; they will be "backed into." Remember the GPS analogy? The end result, or the destination, *forces the hows*.

As you may be sensing, the really great news here is that pictures in your mind of desired end results, particularly when shared by more than one person, and of course when later acted upon, are exactly the means by which you can spark major transformations in your life on earth. Seemingly magical and miraculous, yet you're merely harnessing the energies that have always been at your disposal, manipulating the illusions of the world to match your intentions and expectations.

Your physical senses show you only the resulting probabilities *that were chosen*. They show only the yield of what your prior thoughts, beliefs, and actions have led to. If you want to spark change in your life in a positive way, you need to change your understanding of life's mechanics, imagine your life as if the changes you seek have already taken place, and begin acting as if those changes are now reality to any degree possible, in spite of contradictory appearances. *Et voilà*, enjoy your new life on earth.

Not a single one of the people involved in a 200,000-death natural disaster was there by accident. Everyone was there for their own divine and perfect reasons, as a reflection of their thoughts, beliefs, and intents.

And what of those who didn't die, but who now suffer physically and emotionally—why?

Of course it's not only people's deaths that are exquisitely timed and orchestrated in harmony when seen on a time line by their greater selves, based upon their thoughts, beliefs, and expectations; *no second of any day is any less sacred*. Every stubbed toe, every cancer, and every good or wonderful or boring or unpleasant occurrence that ever happens to you is similarly "blessed," and by inference, is what *you've* ordained.

But why would someone want anything unpleasant to happen to themselves?

Actually, in terms of the event itself, virtually *no one* would; however, in terms of the experience that would come from the event, *everyone* would. For instance, there are countless cancer survivors who view the experience as one of the greatest "gifts" of their life. Do you think they're talking about the hideous disease that destroyed cells and required chemotherapy? No. Nobody wants that. Nobody wants to suffer. Nobody wants to cry. But stand back from the equation, and, hypothetically, cancer can be seen to create all kinds of fringe benefits. It can bring members of a family that had been irreconcilably separated back together for a reunion, appreciation, and a brand-new start. The cancer is gone, the relationships are improved—what a blessing!

Someone who, hypothetically, felt powerless in the physical world, but having been afflicted with cancer, battled it, and then beat it, may suddenly discover their power. The cancer is gone, their power remains—what a blessing!

Or cancer might spark a renewed appreciation for life in the person who's simply weary, jaded, or in a rut. When they hear, "I'm sorry. You've got about six months to live," they might see life on earth in an entirely new light. Jolted into an appreciation that wasn't there before. After a battle, the cancer's beaten, and the appreciation remains—what a blessing!

What of the people who don't beat cancer?

Again, *everybody beats cancer*, in this lifetime or beyond. Nobody dies—not ever. If they've transitioned, they're still adventuring with the same personality, with the same zest (or distaste, at least until they learn better) for life. In their case it was "their time," as always, determined by their cumulative thoughts, beliefs, and expectations, evidenced by their departure. The choice of cancer, though not usually conscious, is motivated by a different reason for every single person who has it, although, often, part of the reason (in the case of those departed) is to have a bit more time on earth than a quick death would offer. Whether to say their good-byes, to prepare the paperwork, the wills, the trust, to make sure everything is taken care of. Others may feel, "I don't need any of that. I don't care. I want it to be quick. I want to be out of here and on my way." These are personal choices, intentional or not, factored in with all else they think, dream of, and fear, with consideration given to the survivors they'll leave behind.

So, we needn't feel sympathy for those traumatically affected by natural disasters? They created them, they needed them, let them have their lesson?

Hardly! Remember, if you're even aware of the disaster, it means that to a degree, however minuscule, you also had a role in its creation. Why?

As just recounted, one of the reasons people may participate in a natural disaster globally or privately is for the effect it will have on the survivors around them. In other words, sometimes the "victim" might choose to be the "victim" (better to call them heroes in this light) in part to create opportunities for Good Samaritans to learn of their own power through giving comfort or assistance. Samaritans who would otherwise not have experienced the difference they could make. For example, seeing the horrific images of innocent civilians and children maimed or killed when war comes to their city spurs many an individual and nation, from far corners of the globe, to *finally do something for their hurt and fallen brothers and sisters*, if only to donate money. These catastrophes are an invitation to wake up and be involved. It's never a matter of saying, "Oh, I happened to see on the news today . . ." If you saw it, there was a reason it caught your attention, and that reason might just be to treasure your own life more, if not to get on a plane and render assistance. If one person on a planet of One-expressing-as-many suffers, all suffer. If you can ease the suffering of one person, you will have eased it for the rest as well.

So, similarly, just as you would comfort a child who was lost or sick, even though their predicament was of their own creation, so, too, is there abundant reason and cause to offer comfort and support to adults who find themselves in need of help.

You mean to tell me that little children choose to die or become orphans from natural disasters?!

Same answer applies: no matter their age, it was part of their own "plans and intents." Your concern stems from thinking that children are all new souls, here by "accident," with no say in the circumstances of their life. Not true. As explained at length earlier, you're all ancient spiritual gladiators who've brilliantly planned the stage of your present life "before" it even began, fully aware of the probabilities that may likely unfold. Every child's higher self knew and chose the times they'd be born into, as well as all of the other parameters of their lives. These choices are all based on the kind of adventures they're partial to, where and what their friends are choosing, and the kind of things they want to learn and experience. No one chooses to be born in order to, at the age of three years, two months, and four days, drown in a tidal wave. Life is not preordained, and all "destinies" are malleable; only probabilities exist that are then narrowed down according to changing individual and mass thoughts. These kids fully understood that they were choosing to be born into primitive times, when systems and technologies (and mind-sets) might not prevent them from being in harm's way, and when the mass consciousness might find it useful (for a million and one reasons) to be pummeled by Mother Nature. And once they were born, as their young lives unfolded and mass probabilities became more and more focused, all of their thoughts weighed together with their parents' or guardians', and everyone was in exactly the right place at the right time, during the "unexpected" flooding.

Whether or not you can see it, there is always order, hope, meaning, healing, and love in every second of every day in every life on earth.

There's another unfortunate misconception that's implied by your question, and that is that any death, particularly of a child, means there were opportunities lost. "They'll never walk down the aisle. They'll never have their first job. They'll never . . ." The list is endless, but each "They'll never" reveals a blindness to the fact that when the door to this particular life on earth closes, another one flies open, angels sing, and choirs erupt—and a whole new adventure begins. The child, or the young adult, or the aged adult who passes away has just started a brand-new journey that's even more perfect for them, based on where their thinking lies, than the one they've just been on. Would you think of it as a lost opportunity if a child became a teacher instead of an engineer, or vice versa? No, instead you'd respect whatever their choice was, knowing it would be filled with its own opportunities, and the same can be true in the case of an unexpected death.

Granted, it may be easier and more comforting to think there's evil in the world and bad things happen to good people for no reason, but these outgrown ideas actually hurt you more in the long run. They deprive you of the peace that only truth can offer. Truth frees you from guilt and the massive suffering that comes from believing in eternally lost opportunities. No explanation will put a smiley face on the death of a child or an adult, or upon anything that is experienced as ugly, painful, or disturbing. But whether or not you can see it, there is always order, hope, meaning, healing, and love in every second of every day in every life on earth.

In case you're still convinced it's inhumane to take these views, at least don't equate the quest to understand phenomena with a desire to justify them. Just as doctors' understanding of diseases, their ability to explain their causes and effects, does not mean they consider the diseases "justified," neither will your new insights mean you are justifying the ugly, painful, or disturbing.

One last thing. Just because a life may end, seemingly before it has begun, does not mean that it has not been an experience worth having for the child and for those who loved her. One's final moments need not, and do not, characterize a life. They are but moments.

But why would someone choose to be born into a poor or dangerous country or to have ignorant parents?

Again, infinite reasons, all easier to accept when you realize that you can choose to live as many lives as you want, wherever and as whoever you want, and knowing this, combined with the fact that life in time and space is "just a dream" from which all awaken unscathed, unharmed, and as "more" than who they were before it began. It should then make perfectly good sense that you would choose a variety of lives with a variety of challenges and opportunities, rather than just being born, time and again, gorgeous, talented, rich, and spoiled.

This is in keeping with *your* adventurous nature. You wanted it all! Not just the sanitized, G-rated family edition. Being born into the lap of luxury for seven and a half thousand lifetimes would definitely get old. No adventure! After each lifetime you'd be reminiscing and looking back at how everything was just given to you, where you hardly stretched for anything before Mom or Dad put a silver spoon in your mouth or gave you exactly what it was you wanted. Meanwhile you'd be watching other adventurers arrive from their recent lives. "This one came from a hut or a tribe in the Congo! And these two came from Manhattan, where they navigated enormous social and corporate realms! This one lived on a fishing ship in the Indian Ocean!" and so on. There'd be tales among you of, "I didn't have!" "I did have!" "I wanted!" "I got!" "I was afraid!"" I overcame!" and you'd be like, "Man, my life really sucked. All I had was Wi-Fi and fancy cars for seven and a half thousand lifetimes. I wish I could have had a little bit of what they had."

Adventure is not about eternally living your life in the lap of luxury; it is most certainly not about "easy"! While you tend to think people born in third-world nations drew the short straw, how do you know they don't pity the "poor" people who live in first-world nations, who never learn community, family, and connection, and who live lives locked in competition, mostly indoors, desperate to prove their value through outward displays of productivity? Which is not to say that there aren't parts of the world that surely seem to breed misery, but not nearly to the degree that you think, and still, it would always be for the adventure.

Also consider, being born to naïve or uneducated parents will give you an adventure that you could *never* have if you were born of Harvard-educated parents. And since you're eternal and since you choose as many lives as you want, again it makes some sense you'd want to mix things up. Right? You're like that. Go ahead and have the Beverly Hills life, and then when that bores you silly, get ready for some real adventure, which may, however, at times come with the rare and unusual price of probabilities that might include being wiped off the earth due to Mother Nature.

Lastly, consider that many if not most of the things you value now, today, are assuredly not going to be the things you value when you have a much higher perspective.

OK, if I agreed with all that other stuff, I could see how diversity would be a boon. But, for example, to be abused or even raped as a child . . . How can you explain the truly disturbed life?

Millions of reasons, and you can have the "disturbed" label. First of all, wouldn't you expect that there *are* answers? Doesn't it make more sense that there would be order, perfection, and love beneath every event that happens within a loving, intelligent Universe, than not? After all, everything is actually happening "inside" of God, remember? There is no "outside."

Clearly there are existences that from virtually every angle appear to be truly offensive and horrifically sad. Yet even so, when standing far enough back from the equation, in every such situation, you can sense there is order, perfection, and love involved.

Hypothetically: What if there were a particular soul you loved more than words could say, together with whom you'd adventured and rampaged and loved throughout countless millennia? Yet there comes a time when your beloved begins journeys down paths you were scared of, unfamiliar with, and uninterested in. So in the spirit of setting free that which you long to hold, you let them go down such paths as you lovingly await their promised return.

To your shock and dismay, you watch as your loved one journeys so far, and into such inhospitable territory, that you see him become lost in rage, fury, and fear. To the point that violence becomes his primary means for dealing with life on earth.

Rather than returning to you as hoped and expected, he becomes so utterly terrified that in between these crazy and lost lifetimes, he even *forgets who you are*, though you remain as in love with him as you have ever been. He hasn't changed, only his perceptions of reality, and hence his reactions to it.

Brokenhearted and filled with a soulful desire to help, watching this all unfold from a place of peace and compassion, surrounded by loving guides, you are shown a way you *can* help. You see that if you would be willing to cross paths with your beloved again on the physical plane, to be born as his daughter in an upcoming life, despite his altered state, in the instant he first laid eyes on you as a crying babe, he'd be gripped by love, though he'd know not why.

But you're also shown that in this same incarnation, even as much as he would love you, probabilities would exist in which he might be prone to uncontrollable fits of anger and violence, and these at times might be directed at you in vile and traumatic ways. Yet with every such trespass and violation, he would, for the first time in all of his "misguided" lifetimes without you, begin to understand the destructive and futile nature of his violent ways. Only by directing his violence at you, his beloved of countless lifetimes, would he be sure to see this, and it could lead to his greatest and most transformational healing since the two of you parted.

If this was what you were shown, and you knew that whatever ended up happening in this possible dream life of yours among the illusions of time and space, you'd still return whole and complete to a place of peace and compassion, surrounded again by loving guides, would you choose to help? Would you volunteer? Choose to risk your young life, even though in grander terms you could only gain? That no matter what happened, you would be greater for it? That you may even rescue your cherished companion in this one bold move?

You would. It's just a dream.

You cannot be all that you dream of being if you believe in random bad stuff happening to folks for no reason.

Yet, even as you're reading this now, tomorrow you may catch a sad or revolting story on the news that has viewers wondering, "How could this happen in the world if there's a God?" Of course, you wouldn't see the full, spiritual picture, just the hideous tip of the iceberg. At least now, however, while you will never know of all the intricacies, reasons, calculations, and intentions that permeated the tragedy, you can grasp that they exist, and you can know that love and the desire to heal were present. This does not justify it, nor does it mean there shouldn't be an outpouring of compassion for the hurt, nor criminal prosecutions and ideally rehabilitation for violators, and whatever else your society normally deems appropriate in the circumstances.

This just got weird. What happened to life's magic, its beauty, and our power?

If you want power, you must have understanding. You cannot be all that you dream of being if you believe in random bad stuff happening to folks for no reason. There are only miracles, and if you can now comprehend what's been offered and thereby erase even one more question you had regarding life on earth, you will rest that much quicker upon your rightful throne as a conscious and deliberate creator, overseeing your kingdom where always, everywhere, there is order, healing, and love.

And consider, you don't usually have to deal with natural disasters daily, weekly, or even yearly. In fact, most people will never experience a natural disaster in their entire lifetime! Sure, accidents and setbacks can show up daily, even hourly, but for the reasons given, these are always setups for greatness—so if they arrive daily or hourly, how "lucky" for you. Moreover, and far more important, is to understand that just as a "once-in-a-blue-moon" catastrophe can occur, individually and for a greater population, all due to underlying thoughts, beliefs, intentions, *and only where probabilities permit it*, so do great bursts of creativity, causes for celebration, spiritual evolution, and joyful, planetary transformation. This is the norm for life on earth, where virtually everyone has at least 10,000 times more reasons to be happy than sad.

Both your thoughts and the probabilities must align for anything to happen. Rarely is this even possible in terms of disasters, which is why there are so few. Whereas it's almost always possible in terms of enjoying your life, growing, expanding, and being loved. The same forces that can, on rare occasions, send destructive tidal waves flowing, are available to everyone, every day, the world over, to create fantastic individual and collective change.

Hold on. Getting back to me . . . I still don't quite know who is driving the bus in my life. You've said that "thoughts becoming things is as predictable as gravity," and you've also said that our higher selves, life's magic, Divine Intelligence, and the Universe help bring our dreams to pass. Which is it? What if I want something, but my higher self thinks I need a tidal wave? Who wins?

To clarify the notion of your higher self: You are more than you can now comprehend. A multidimensional, living, and expanding God. You are *right now* actively involved in other lifetimes, in the past, future, and other realms. You're also all "One," so it could be fairly said that you are within every other person who has ever lived, is now living, and will ever live. And then there is a "higher version" of yourself who chose this lifetime, which you recall nothing of, and "higher" versions still. Don't even try to comprehend all of this, except to realize that if we are to talk about you, we need a way of referring to *which* you we're speaking of to make certain points.

So we can now say a "higher you," which is still pure you, chose to be who you now think you are. The decision to be today's "you" was made, not just to experience human passions, lessons, and emotions, but to see what would happen as the person you will "design" and choose to be. Just as you often find your present life to be a mystery-puzzle-game-to-be-strategized-and-won, so can you choose to see lifetimes like this before choosing their parameters. In each lifetime you choose your parents (and they you), the guidance or lack of guidance you'll probably receive, the era, places, even neighborhood (if relevant), as well as your leanings and inclinations, like the levels of creativity you'll possess. Will you be left- or right-brain inclined? Good with your hands? The arts? Sciences? Plus, you'll factor in all the traits, skills, and hard-earned disciplines acquired cumulatively in all of your prior lives that you'll bring to bear. All to see what will happen—to see what you will do with it once your life gets going, to see how you will react to the world, to see the goals you will choose and how you will move toward them, to see what you will question, what you will answer, what you'll fear, who you'll befriend, and on and on and on, ad infinitum. Why? Because you can! Because it's fun! Because you'll always be safe! Because everything that might happen and everything that might not will add to who you'll be for eternity!

The choice to be here is made at this "higher" level, which is not to imply "better" level, just "other" level. All other choices beyond that, from the point each life physically begins, are entirely made at "street level," where the mortal you meets your illusions. Some choices are intentional, but until the full truth is known about your thoughts becoming things, most will be unintentional.

Other than being here as you, your higher self has no agenda, and, thus, does not wish for you anything that could ever be in contradiction to what you are wishing for you. Even desires of yours that might seem shallow, childish, or hurtful are not contradicted. What better way to learn of your own misunderstandings than to want and manifest "things" that will truly not bring you joy, all contained in an illusionary world, from which everyone returns safe and sound? And it's not just that there will never be contradictions; the truth is that as your life unfolds, both street-level and higher-level "yous" are synchronized; here, there really is only one you! What the street-level you desires on earth is what the higher-level you wants as you! You are one and the same.

In other words, the higher-level you *wanted* to live among the illusions with blinders on, with total amnesia, in order to find "his" way, know himself, and discover life's truths anew. Why? Because "he" could; again, because it would be "fun." So "he" is here now, as you. You are him, here, with blinders on, at street level. You think for him, speak for him, decide everything for him; *you are him*. Contradictions are impossible. There is only what you want, never what your higher self wants for you, other than your presence here to begin with.

Finally, to help you really get this, let's say you, today, at street level, are experiencing wanderlust, and you decide to visit faraway and exotic Kathmandu for the first time in your life. Right? Why? Because you can, because it would be fun to see what happens! So, after months of preparations and planning, finally the time comes when you actually find yourself walking the sloped alleys and old temples of the town, and then you come to a fork in the road, at which you weigh instinct, knowledge, and eye-appeal to decide upon the direction you'll go. Would you also wonder what the "you" back home six months ago would have chosen? Would you worry about contradicting her? No, a pretty ridiculous idea, right? Right.

But you said my higher self, or life's magic, or whatever, would work out "the details." What gives?

Concerning "the details" of every manifestation being worked out by life's magic, Divine Intelligence, the Universe, or your higher self: To be clear, any such references are simply to empha-size that such machinations, calculations, and determinations are not done, can't be done, shouldn't be worried about, by street-level you. They are not meant to imply, although they admittedly do, that there is another mind, independent of yours, subjectively giving or taking opportunities from you and others. In fact, the metaphysical principle of *thoughts becoming things*, like any principle of physics, *flows* with an automatic, natural, flawless precision. It isn't "activated" any more than gravity is "activated." It's always on. And just as gravity could be said to "help" a boulder find the fastest path down the mountain, so do your thoughts "know how" to find their fastest way into your life on earth—although in neither case is there any real decision-making happening, just the effortless, spontaneous forces of nature working themselves out among all of the elements.

The implication that manifestations are being "worked out elsewhere" offers a gentle bridge for connecting the old worldview of a subjective God, deciding who gets what and when, to a more accurate representation of what happens. In actuality, there's no subjectivity involved. Not on the part of an angry God with a scorecard, or even a benign Universe who dotes upon you. The physical world simply mirrors your thoughts, beliefs, and expectations, and mirrors don't lie or pass judgment. They just are. Life's only subjectivity lies with you and how you interpret, feel, imagine, or react to your creations, whether or not you even know they are your creations. And therein lies the adventure! The only difference between glass mirrors and the mirror of the physical world is that the first offers spontaneous reflections, whereas life on earth, through the constructs of time and space, requires patience for your new thoughts to add themselves into the physical mosaic of all your other thoughts, and those of your co-creators.

You can, accordingly, sense and know that everything that happens in anyone's life, from the point of birth onward, is the fluid, streaming reflection of everyone's contribution to their shared manifestations, from their street-level minds, though necessarily taking into account the relevant decisions that have brought them to wherever they are in the present moment (who their parents are, height, skin color, where they went to school, who they married, etc.).

Is there any chance I won't ultimately prevail? Is there any chance I won't one day return to the "place" from which this all began?

Imagine, hypothetically, before you ever took the big plunge into time and space, you were considering your options:

You were gazing into eternity, filled with the power and freedom to do whatever you wanted with it.

One day, as you pondered your infinite options, a friend came along and said, "Hey! How about we go to the jungles of time and space? It's the latest craze! Thrilling! Terrifying! It's where we can go to fleetingly forget that we're everywhere, always at once!"

Shocked but intrigued, you asked, "If I choose to go, will anything bad happen to me?"

"No, no, no, no, nothing bad will happen to you . . . except, well, there, people believe they die at the end of their lives. Scary, sure, but harmless. Snap, crackle, pop, and *the real you* will be not-dead again. Before you die, however, you'll be innately inclined to succeed, with the power to change your circumstances on the fly, and love will abound wherever you go . . . though sometimes you won't see it."

"Well, is there a chance that I won't get to return here?"

"Oh my gosh, no, no, no, no. That's impossible! In fact, the whole drama will actually be played out 'here,' but you'll think you're 'there.'"

"Will help always be available? Will friends always be nearby? Will I still possess supernatural powers?"

"Oh, heck yeah! *Your thoughts will become things and your words will give you wings!* Once of God, always of God! And the place is teeming with angels who will get involved whenever you so much as say, 'Ouch!'"

And so you got "in line" for your turn in space. And you'd have waited in line for a million years to have the chances *you now have*, to be who you are now, to believe in this fiction so that you could have such bold and daring, thrilling and terrifying adventures, which would all be of your own creation, as you play out your life, metaphorically, in the palm of God's hand.

Right here, right now, you literally possess the eyes and ears of God. You are the face of Divinity come alive in the dream of time and space. Show compassion to those suffering in the lands of war and chaos. Show compassion to those suffering due to natural disasters. Show compassion to *everyone*, because they're your spiritual brothers and sisters. And with this kind of open heart and the willingness to engage life, good things become better things, and they'll happen in your life faster and faster and faster—not because you will be judged worthy, but because your vibe will be in harmony with the true nature and abundance of life.

CHAPTER 7

SHOW ME THE MONEY

I think this stuff might agree with me

Can anyone become a money magnet?

Why does it seem that unspiritual people usually make the most money?

What if this was supposed to be someone's "poor" life so they could learn to go without?

Selfish . . . me . . . what if I am?

Could you give me a cheat sheet, steps to take, or something more like an action plan to make more money?

Does giving really lead to receiving?

If thoughts become things, why isn't everyone rich?

Moving the conversation to something more "green" than accidents, setbacks, and disasters, can we talk about money? As
in, how can I get more of it? Is that OK? To want money? For
myself?

It's time you outgrew the guilt that comes from misunderstanding selfishness. Earlier we talked about honoring the individual. This includes financially. There's nothing wrong with
aspiring to the freedom money can give you, nor, for that matter,
aspiring to possess money itself. Selfishness is nothing more than
an expression of the Divine through you, and a celebration of life's
possibilities. So go ahead, want it all. *That's what it's there for!*

You might be surprised to know your world is actually evolving away from an era that mistakenly put an overemphasis on the
collective and an underemphasis on the individual. This imbal-
ance was supposed to be a more spiritual approach to priorities—
living for the needs of others—even while those encouraging it,
namely, religious and political leaders, were generally not. They
were people of power with an agenda, who wanted to use guilt
as a tool of manipulation, asking individuals to dampen the very
passions that excited them most—the pursuit of their own happiness—for the sake of enriching the collective, and themselves.

Yet a collective has neither heart to love nor spirit to be loved.
Nor mind to understand the characters of the people within it.
The people, the individual members of any group, become the
collective, but they never cease being individuals. When members
naturally honor their "feelings of incompleteness" they become
passionately motivated to go in directions that will minimize
their fears and suffering while improving their health and happiness, adding to and supporting the lives of others in the same
ways, and therefore truly helping the so-called collective.

It's important that you no longer view this approach to life as
"selfish" in the way selfishness is usually defined: pursuing self-
interests *at the expense of others*; being overly indulgent, uncar-
ing, and greedy. Just think about this older definition of the word
and you'll see its failings. If you make progress at the expense of

anybody you love or care about, burn bridges between yourself and your partner, your family, your employer, or your community, are you really making progress? Won't it *always* come back to haunt you? Which becomes especially clear when you understand that "thoughts become things." If such is your vibe, you will attract others of the same vibe. And what you now know of your eternal nature means your vibe and its repercussions will follow you beyond this lifetime, so it's not as if what you "get away with" in this lifetime will just be water under the bridge—not until you change your vibe.

Go ahead, want it all.
That's what it's there for!

So, consider, if you're supposedly trying to make progress with *this kind* of selfish approach, ripping off others and then being ripped off yourself, you will not make any net headway. And, thus, it is not motivated by a *true* selfish interest, but by spiritual *stupidity*, if I may say so.

Everyone, given the nature of the earlier-described sense of incompletion, yearns to grow, move ahead, go bigger, run faster, and live longer, as well as to love and be loved—not to be hated and smited. In this way, everyone is naturally selfish. It's a by-product of the Divine within you, the spark of God that seeks eternal growth and expansion, and it means all of your actions would automatically take into consideration your loved ones and, to a great degree, humanity at large. Yet the person who thinks they can expand their experience at the expense of others simply demonstrates ignorance, offsetting their natural *inclination* to succeed.

Moreover, as earlier reviewed, the truth is always known. So, in this lifetime, or just beyond when you're having a final life review, when everybody is seeing the truth of everyone else, and all see that you pulled 10 people "under," thinking it was how you would get ahead . . . *awkward*, to say the very least. And even before that final life review, you'll be a long way from happiness, as you'll live in constant fear that someone will do to you what you have been doing to others, since you obviously believe you live in a world where such behavior is an acceptable option. This is biting your nose to spite your face, not realizing that you are all connected. Not realizing that in an illusionary world, there's enough for everyone, and you don't have to get yours by cheating, stealing, or misleading.

Selfishness, rightly played, is a holy thing. It just needs to be spiritually understood with a recognition that you will be your best and give the most when you honor your dreams, *which include your natural desire to do well by those you love, humanity, and the world*; that helping to put smiles on their faces, rather than frowns, will behoove your own happiness and serve your own interests as much as theirs.

But are there more spiritual dreams than the dream of having more money? Am I being too materialistic?

Everything is spirit, material things all the more so because they've been thought about and believed in so much that they've shown up! The notion that people with money aren't spiritual is simply not a "rule." Just look at what you could do with lots of money. Is it unspiritual to have raised $10 million, so that you could give $2 million to a charity serving the hungry? Isn't this spreading the wealth *and the love*? What if you used your money to set up college scholarships for your children and grandchildren? Or to take them on international trips to witness firsthand different cultures around the planet? Or to create a business and employ people while accumulating wealth for your family? Or, after a great run of 5, 10, or 20 years as an investor-entrepreneur, to incorporate your own nonprofit organization that brings technology, computers, and the Internet to underdeveloped parts of the world? Not that you even have to give *anything* away; there's nothing wrong with making tons of money just because doing so makes you happy.

These are freedoms that only money offers. Not that wonderful things can't also be done without money, and, of course, you can definitely be happy without it. It's your life, your prerogative to pursue abundance or not. Either way, it's time to clear up the notion that material wealth is somehow not spiritual.

How is it that sometimes the least spiritual people seem to create the most wealth?

First, your question, as it was literally posed, presumes there are "unspiritual" people. There are not. The question is fatally flawed because everyone is spiritual. There's no condition in the world, nor person upon it, that is not some form of the Divine expressing. It's all spiritual.

Second, your question again implies there is or should be some sort of judgment that decides who gets what. *There is no celestial or divine judgment of life on earth* whatsoever, except your own, and yours is fine, until it makes you unhappy. And knowing this, you remove from your pathway to wealth one of the biggest stumbling blocks of all—the idea that you must be found worthy by some estimation of "God."

Finally, whether you call those who've behaved poorly unkind or unspiritual (the former is possible), at least you've noticed the evidence that there's no "good behavior test" to pass for living in abundance. Pretty cool. You are loved. You're already as good as you need to be. You've already paid your dues, and living in your jungles is living in the winner's circle of creation, no matter how you behave here.

What if I chose this lifetime to experience lack, poverty, and doing without?

Believing in destiny, fate, or karma as absolutes throws your power out the window. There are likelihoods and probabilities, period. Nothing is set in stone, other than what you "write" in thought, belief, and expectation. And even then, you can change your mind. Within those same limiting ideas, however, are more deceptive distractions, like the notion of purpose, life's mission, dharma, or what it is you are supposed to be doing with your life. *Deciding.* That's it. You are there to decide what to do with your life, and to do it. You have certain strengths, interests, and desires—follow those. Not to your destiny, but as tips to where the most fun and learning may lie for you. That's why you're alive. To see what comes of that bold decision to plunge into the jungles of time and space.

There is no celestial or divine judgment of life on earth whatsoever, except your own.

No one has ever chosen a *lifetime* to know suffering. Why would they? God goes where God wants to go, and no one wants to just starve to death any more than they want to have their head banged with a hammer. They might choose, however, a stage to be born onto where there would be challenges, maybe severe, life-threatening challenges, but there would always be other reasons as well, like love, family, community, learning, growing, and/ or fun. And while you could point to lives lived by the poorest, where you see none of these redeeming qualities, or to children, babies even, whose lives were snuffed out so fast they knew only pain, that would hardly be proof that redeeming qualities were absent, nor that these individuals' objectives weren't met. You live in a world of the Divine, by the Divine, for the Divine, and there is always order, meaning, purpose, and above all love involved with every choice to be born onto any stage. Accordingly, you carry with you the great likelihood of realizing success, financially and in all other ways.

It just can't be that easy! Everybody would be rich if it were.

First, while this will be hard for any Western mind to grasp, not everybody wants to be rich. Second, thinking that making money is very hard *makes* it very hard. Like all beliefs, this one becomes a self-fulfilling prophecy. Odd, however, that evidence to the contrary of "making money is hard" is everywhere! Today, you should know, on your planet there are 17,000,000 millionaires and almost 2,000 *billionaires*! Rich folk abound, on every continent. And consider, in most countries you do not have to have anywhere near a million dollars to be considered fabulously wealthy. So, how hard can making money be? Drop the belief and watch your fortunes change.

If there's a predominant focus on poverty and lack, whether from concern or fear, as you focus, you create, perpetuate, and decree. Or, similarly, if when you talk about material prosperity, you choose phrases like, "Making money takes luck." "You have to be in the right place at the right time." "It's not what you know but who you know." "Only the early bird gets the worm." "Opportunity only knocks once." Such statements become the bars of the jail you must then live behind. Bars you put in place.

Opportunity *never stops* knocking. You live in a dream world, remember? In fact, if you were to come into your own first million dollars in the months ahead, it's such small news that your local media probably wouldn't even pick up the story. "So what?!" To get there yourself, to first have the mind-set of abundance, you just have to know the truth about the nature of reality—that you're the dreamer of your life on earth—and then begin "showing up" every day, taking action in the direction of amassing wealth, even when it seems futile and you feel like nothing is happening. There's nothing hard about it, except it requires taking action that seems futile while dreaming of champagne and caviar. It's this seeming futility that stops most people from showing up. But this juxtaposition is what makes life an adventure; this is life's hook again. Ironically, those on the sidelines, who idolize the ones making fortunes, know not how easy it was for them, so they tell stories of their heroes that reinforce the lie that making money is very difficult. The rich are happy to believe it. Everyone reinforces it. And then—TBT, *thoughts become things*—to those who have, more is given; from those who lack, more is taken—because this is their focus!

So, if I just adopt the correct mind-set, I'll become a money magnet?

It depends what you mean by mind-set. If you mean to make vision boards, repeat mantras, visualize, read wise books, have enlightened friends, then no.

If you add to this mix, however, *doing* new things, regularly, at least weekly, to move toward abundance, you will indeed become a money magnet.

If one's mind-set were to really, deeply change, they would automatically be taking action, new action, on their dreams. This is what understanding does for you, clears up all confusion and contradiction, revealing that the Universe can't do all it can unless you do all you can. Knowing this, you show up daily, doing stuff. Lots of stuff. Almost anything goes, as long as it makes sense to you and is your best effort working with what you have from where you are *toward what you want*. With a glad heart, not insisting on or attaching to the results of any particular effort, but working lots of different angles, trying lots of different things, having faith that ultimately one of them will lead you in the correct direction for, in this case, living in abundance. The idea of "thoughts becoming things" has always implied that words and actions will be congruent with the thoughts in question.

So, what might you imagine is the easiest way for anyone to just show up? I'll give you a hint: to many people, it's a four-letter word.

"Work!" Yes, the thing people do who don't know how to fish, as the bumper stickers say.

"Me? Work? No way. I've seen *The Secret*—I'm just going to receive checks in the mail and retire! Besides, the pay was lousy, it was a dead-end job, and I felt trapped. Working for other people doesn't agree with me."

Yet these feelings stem from how you all too often *choose* to view work. As if it's supposed to be the be-all and end-all of how our magical life takes off, yet only pays $9 per hour. Anyone would *rightfully* feel disillusioned and on the wrong path if this was how they viewed work. Instead, choose differently.

What if you saw work as one of your most exciting dances with life? One that changes and evolves in magical ways over the years? What you do and where you do it would be transitory, but the fact that you'd be doing something would be ongoing. Instead of seeing it as a way to "pay your dues," you'd see it as a chance to meet a parade of new people, some who'd become best friends. A place to discover your own untested potentials and unpolished gifts, to be of service to the world, and to create possibilities for abundance to find you. Not the be-all and end-all, but merely a baby step; as in hoisting your sails so the Universe can fill them, making yourself a lightning rod for miracles and serendipities. Not to mention the office parties, donut runs, and free pens.

Just as "objects in mirror are closer than they appear," deliberate manifestations are inevitably greater than you thought they'd be.

With abundance as your end result, through baby steps that include work *and all other ideas you may have* for moving in abundance's direction, the magic is unleashed. It probably won't be visible in a day. Probably not even in a week or a month, maybe not even in a year or two, but that won't mean it's not working. It might take four years; remember, you have big dreams. But when it finally does show up, you're going to say, "Dang, that was fast!" "Wow, that was easy!" "It was totally meant to be! I always knew I'd arrive at this 'place.'" Guaranteed. And then, of course, as you know, your life and success will be even better than you imagined they would be. Just as "objects in mirror are closer than they appear," deliberate manifestations are inevitably greater than you thought they'd be.

Still sounds too easy . . .

Nothing could be easier than living in a world where your thoughts become things . . . as long as you know what all of your

60,000 thoughts per day are, none are in contradiction, and the beliefs that give rise to those thoughts are empowering, abundant, and preferably rooted in the Truths of Being. Right, *not so easy* if you chose to be born into these primitive times, but still far easier than your believed-in and much-valued approach of "blood, sweat, and tears," which is still thought to require some luck and connections.

It's not that making money is hard—it's not. It's in getting a hold of the truth concerning your reality, and then working that truth, all in spite of the entire world thinking otherwise, and your own past evidencing otherwise, that the challenge emerges. Challenge, meaning adventure! You can so do this, and think of the payoff . . . cash! Millions! Plus, friends, laughter, and love! Healing, good looks, and mobility! All that your heart now desires! Just like where you came from, pre–time and space, from which you wanted "more." Which is to say you wanted things to be exactly as they now are in your life, and you knew what you were doing! Not so they would stay the way they now are, but so that you could change them!

What if making a million bucks was "easy" in the way you think you want it to be, and *everyone* could do it? What if owning a luxury car was "easy," and everyone had one? What if growing a business was "easy," and everyone grew one? Would these things have the same appeal to you? YOU? No, not you. *Easy* is not appealing. *Common* is not appealing. You probably can't even imagine how awful your life would be if you won the lottery every weekend, if every room you entered people fawned all over you, and if every door you knocked upon revealed another Prince or Princess Charming. YUCK! You wanted it all, the Full Monty, the real, raw deal. You are not in the jungles of time and space because you wanted "easy." Although now that you're here, and everyone has you believing that life is hard and people are mean, *"easy" sure looks good*. Forget it. Drill down to truth. Know who and where you are, *get* these mechanics of manifestation, and your every accomplishment, friend, and victory will become all the sweeter, especially given the primitive mentality you now live in.

Do you know what's better than getting to the "top of the mountain"? Getting there after having been lost.

This all sounds good, but thoughts, words, and actions are sometimes hard to keep track of. Could I have a cheat sheet, tips, or steps to take?

How about "Twenty-One Steps for Opening the Floodgates of Abundance in the Jungles of Time and Space"?

Are there, really?

Step 1: Dream! Define your desired end result, your desired abundant lifestyle! This is what you already tell your children: "Dream, because dreams do come true!" And it's because you instinctively know it's true. Thoughts become things. So it's incumbent upon you to start dreaming again, and because it matters to you, specifically about abundance. Financial wealth and freedom. Imagine the nuances of a life lived in luxury. Make a list of details about the house and where it's going to be and the roof it's going to have and whether or not you've got a view of the woods or a lake or the mountains—get into the specifics. List, list, list, list! Define abundance in *your terms.* Not *how* you're going to create it, but what your life will be like *after you have it.* Where are you going to go? Who are you going to go there with? What's going to be your first new hobby? What will be your *next* dream?

Step 2: Visualize daily. It's the least you can do to get the most. If you understand that thoughts become things, this exercise simply gives you the opportunity to deliberately choose and think the kind of thoughts you'd like to physically meet in the world. Give yourself a few minutes every day to think thoughts of living the life of your wildest dreams, as if you were already living it.

Step 3: Create vision boards, scrapbooks, post quotes up around your home. Another way to steer your wandering imagination to the kind of "things" or circumstances you'd like to physically experience in your life: put pictures on your refrigerator, your bathroom mirror, in your purse, in your wallet, in your car. This is just feeding the fire of thoughts becoming things. These props will remind you constantly of "who you really are," as represented by your collection of photos and quotes. Do this; it's not rocket science. You don't need willpower. You just want to become accustomed to redirecting your thoughts, as you reprogram systems you've been oblivious to your whole life, in order to become the black-belt, conscious manifestor you are capable of being.

Step 4: Until you know what to do, master what's before you. What's the alternative? Quit your job and wait? Until you know what you're going to do and you can do it, keep your day job. Not forever! Not to settle for less! But because quitting, to do nothing, would be most unproductive. And since you don't know what to do, quitting to do something else you're uncertain about would be similarly pointless. Under your circumstances, to be clear, not only should you stay put, but you should master what's before you. In other words, keep doing what you're doing, but do it better. This is how to free yourself from it.

Too often those in jobs they hate think no one knows! Whereas, in truth, even the delivery driver who stops by the workplace once every two weeks knows who that person is who hates her job. And no one wants to go near her, much less promote her or give her new assignments. Similarly, everyone knows who's there doing his best, making the most of the situation, and everyone wants a little bit of that person. So, not only does this step keep you reachable by the magic for your presence in the world, but you're making connections, being seen, available, improving who you are, and getting new ideas.

Step 5: Do the obvious, <u>constantly</u> trying new things. If you're at a loss for what exactly to do next, maybe because you're out of work or just starting up something brand-new, consider doing what your peers, others in your shoes, do. Even though they probably know *not* of life's magic. It matters far less *what* you do than *that* you do it, just so you're doing something that makes some logical and intuitive sense to you regarding moving toward abundance. Knowing what you now know of life's mechanics, of your worth and power, and having grand end results, even though you may be doing virtually the same things as your peers, for all of these reasons you *will* get different results. For example, ask for a raise, network, make "cold calls," update your CV or résumé, mingle with appropriate industry groups, further your education, dabble with investing, learn about the arts of buying and selling, create an Internet presence, and so on.

Did you notice the emphasis on *constantly* a moment ago? No matter where you find yourself, you're a creature of change, living in a changing world. You are perpetually having new and evolving desires. It's part of the plan; this is good and healthy. You will continue growing, moving on to "more" and "better" and "new," and after you've mastered the abundance thing, there's going to be "more" and "better" and "new," and, of course, this applies to whatever else you want, in every area of your life. The greatest way to spark new opportunities and possibilities in your life, including those for abundance, is to be constantly trying new and different things. The more you do, the more the Universe can do for you.

Do you know what's better than getting to the "top of the mountain"? Getting there after having been lost.

Step 6: Align your beliefs with abundance. Remember the earlier-mentioned work-around for aligning and installing new beliefs? It went like this:

1. Name as many beliefs as you can that would support you and your dreams, and then

2. behave, in some small way, daily if possible, as if those beliefs were actually yours.

So for abundance, the kind of beliefs that would support you might be: there's enough for everyone, money is pure spirit and can be a noble value for one's time and energy, your thoughts become things, you having "yours" will help others get "theirs," having money will help you support your favorite charities, everything you touch turns to gold, you are always surrounded by wealth and abundance, you are a money magnet, and the like.

Make your list, add to it often, weigh each item in your thoughts again and again until you see their validity and truth. Speak them, claim them, and *act as if they are yours.*

Step 7: See everything you do as a stepping-stone to greatness. Perspectives rule, and you always get to choose what yours will be. It's not settling for less when you go to a job that's not your dream job if you choose to see it as a stepping-stone to "better," to see it as temporary, to see it as enabling the Universe to reach you in ways it couldn't otherwise. This perspective alone will change how you feel each day, improving the opportunities that will, indeed, be drawn to you.

Step 8: For direction, consider all you like and love. Too many people want to be the next version of their favorite rock star, business icon, or sports hero—instead of just being the best version of themselves. You have what *no one else* has, you feel what *no one else* feels, and you can dream of things that *no one else* can dream of—seize this! It's why "God" chose to be you. You are sacred! Necessary! Loved! Be you! And since abundance can come from literally any vocation, as you can readily see the world over, choose among the vocations that resonate with you and make you excited to be alive.

Step 9: Go! Start! Now! Today! Something to understand from the mechanics we've already reviewed for bringing about life changes, is that:

If you want change, you have to physically go first.

You have to change, and that change must start somewhere. So, if you want to live in greater abundance: How will you change and when will you start?

These are two questions that deserve your immediate attention. Remember, knowing the truth is never enough to change your life; you must act on it.

Step 10: Don't attach to details nor insist upon cursed "hows" or "whos." If you dream of acquiring abundance, realize what you want is far more than an amazing car. And it's about far more than a contract, a house, a deal, or a book you want published. These are trinkets that pale in comparison to the importance of the big-picture value of abundance and a rocking life (which is why you want the abundance, ultimately—so your life can rock, right?). The big picture is what you attach to and insist upon. Hold out your cup and demand nothing less than it overflowing. And then, every day, knock on doors, turn over stones, and move in the direction of your inevitable success. If you write, write a lot. Write a poem, write an essay, write a blog, write a book. Be out there circulating every piece of it. If you're in real estate, network, give talks, learn markets, know rates, study sales, read success stories, brush up on your skills.

In all things, let the Universe connect the dots, manage the details, finding the right cars and contracts for you, with the right people, at the right time. By all means, visualize your desired details *as they fit into the mosaic of your abundant, rocking life*, but do not insist upon the details, only upon your rocking life. Visualize the details to get you excited about your end results, not to *be* your end results. You thereby allow room for "even better."

Step 11: Get a little logical. The ironic misconception among newcomers to spiritual awareness is that all they have to do is follow their heart, and the Universe will take care of all else. Yet to neglect the beauty and power of logic would be as foolhardy as neglecting the beauty and power of your heart. The solution is to use both.

Getting a little logical, or even a little practical, is an excellent way to stir up life's magic. With logic you can map out or deduce where your next opportunity may lie, you can go to these hot spots, you can calculate which stone to turn over, you can judge which door to knock upon. Not to over-rely on logic, but to use it to find intellectual peace with your journey and the confidence to know that you're doing what you can with what you have.

To be clear, using your brain isn't about making sure you take the correct steps or that you're in the right place at the right time—too much pressure. It's to help you multiply all of your efforts.

Step 12: Face fears as they arise. Because they will arise and because they won't be yours accidentally.

Dreams, by their nature, are of things you've likely never experienced, which is why you're dreaming them, right? Which means to manifest them, you'll have to go where you've never gone, right? And be who you've never been? Yet going there and being that, you act surprised when the terrain gets a bit uncomfortable. Suddenly, you feel fear, and you think, "Oh, no . . . this is not what I had in mind! Must not be for me! I can't stare down that giant . . . and why should I have to when the Universe loves me and there's a "Law of Attraction"? I think I'll just go home and watch *The Secret* 30 more times in 30 more days!"

The fear is normal. This fear invariably means you're in exactly the right place at the right time, so keep on keeping on, doing whatever you were doing that lured her out of her den! Embrace her. Switch perspectives: "Oh, *there's* my old friend, fear. She always appears when I have something awesome and surprising to learn."

Fear is a tool for revealing you had a chink in your armor that you didn't even know you had, which can now be filled in, buffed down, and made to shine.

Step 13: Playfully prepare the way for your inevitable "arrival." This is when you start playing, as mentioned earlier, acting "as if" your dream is about to come true, or going a step further, acting "as if" it has already come true. This is again urging you to take action, but for an entirely different reason than the baby steps. The baby steps are to put you within reach of the magic you've summoned with your end results. Here, now, you are playing. Pretending there's either imminent transformation or that it's already happened. Your "inner witness" sees this new, unexpected behavior, causing new highways of thought to be blazed in your brain—scientifically

140

known as neural pathways—creating new thought patterns and affirming beliefs that you have about your success.

As an analogy, say you ordered furniture tonight that was to be delivered Thursday morning. What would you do between the time you ordered it and its arrival on Thursday morning? You'd prepare for its *inevitable* arrival. You'd *physically* rearrange your existing furniture to make space for the new. You might buy a new pillow set to accent the new furniture, or a new throw rug. Right? You wouldn't go home after the purchase and start worrying, "What if it never shows up? What will I do? How will I cope?" Of course it's going to show up!

Setbacks are always setups for an even better, more secure manifestation than what you originally knew to ask for.

Behave exactly the same with your dreams right now! Of course they'll show up! You ordered them from a "wise, loving, magical Universe" who's far more capable than a furniture company. Get ready now! Whatever it is you've ordered, *prepare the way.* Have a celebration party. Get the new business cards. Do stuff for its arrival, because it's coming! Even if you can't afford "new furniture" right now, can you afford the "pillow set"? Buy it, make this demonstration, act as if you *knew* you could soon buy the matching "sofa and chairs."

Step 14: Do not judge your progress, or seeming lack thereof, with your physical senses alone. As mentioned in the GPS navigation analogy, your physical senses cannot see the magic and miracles lining up behind the curtains of time and space, just as you can't see your destination with GPS navigation. In both cases, you have to complete the journey, and actually arrive, in order to know the system didn't fail you. Then and only then do all the miracles become apparent. So, just because it may appear you're not making progress toward abundance, or there might be a setback or a challenge, doesn't mean anything's wrong. What's important is that you maintain the vision, in spite of appearances, and continue taking action. Setbacks are always setups for an even better, more secure manifestation than what you originally knew to ask for.

Step 15: Constantly ask for help, guidance, and ideas. Ask anybody and everybody who's ever achieved as you now dream of achieving for help. Don't be afraid. Don't think it's beneath you.

People want to help. They are the Universe in disguise. It truly is lonely at the top, and those who are there, who have seen so many dreams come true they no longer know what to wish for, begin wishing to help others—and the first people they help are those who ask for it.

Step 16: Constantly offer help, guidance, and ideas. Similarly, be there for others. This is not to evoke the sympathy and appreciation of "God." There's no such judgmental entity "out there." Don't be helpful to impress anybody; do it because when you help somebody else, particularly with something you would like help on, you get to be the one who makes a difference in the world, and as a mighty perk, through helping others, you'll suddenly see *yourself* in a brand-new light and far more objectively.

And there's more . . . best of all, by helping others, no matter the capacity, you demonstrate a belief in your "brotherhood," the power of teams, camaraderie, the virtues of love, life's abundance, and that you have the power and ability to help. And those beliefs will be emboldened. Helping others also evidences a *disbelief* in scarcity and vulnerability.

Step 17: Surround yourself with like-minded people (who are aware of the kind of truths in this journal), and if you can, for the purpose of these steps, wealthier people. Their viewpoints, perspectives, and conversations will help align your thoughts and beliefs with those that portray the possession of abundance as "normal." Fear not, however; if you don't have such connections, you will not be handicapped. Neither are you vulnerable to the thoughts of friends, co-workers, or family who think you aren't realistic, who possess lack-mentality, or who are "negative." The other steps listed here are far more than enough to get your floodgates trembling. As always, just do what you can, with what you have, from where you are.

Step 18: Understand you were born to succeed. As you've heard repeatedly, you are here to play and succeed, joyfully and lovingly, in time and space, without limit. Your very nature, being of the Divine, is to flourish in all settings and by every measure. Know this! Let it sink in. Meditate upon it. Immerse yourself in truth: books, CDs, DVDs, and events. While the rest of the world is saying, "You're getting older, you're gaining weight, you're not what you used to be, you're falling apart, and time's almost up," it's time to counter. Happily, given your propensity for success, again it's as if your slightest efforts here will undermine untold years' worth of people-bashing and life-lamenting done by others. Vigilantly read, listen, and watch programs, written, recorded, or live, that will keep you in your spiritual vibe. Regularly refresh your perspectives with messages that inspire, comfort, and love you into the truth.

Step 19: Rest, play, take time off. These steps are not about working longer and harder. They're about being wiser during whatever time you give to creating abundance while living a balanced life.

So, take time off, have fun, nurture your relationships, and apply the concepts and truths you're finding here to every area of your life. By enjoying the journey and giving yourself rewards along the way, you'll also accelerate the arrival of all that your heart now desires, including financial abundance.

Step 20: Be exceedingly fair and aggressively responsible. To be fair and responsible in society is to realize that you are all truly One, that everybody is doing their best, life is more than fair, you are powerful, and through cooperation, all win . . . and so you shall. Reason enough to put your absolute best foot forward.

Anyone who thinks it's OK to skip paying a bill or two or to pay them late, cheat a little on their taxes, lie to vendors, abuse warranties, and the like, will be drawn into a network of other people who operate on the same wavelength.

Step 21: Celebrate often. As you send out joy, your life draws in joy, and the reasons for your joy will multiply. Celebrate that you have what you have, and celebrate in advance for what's coming, materially and ethereally. Celebrate in advance the amazing financial changes that are now sweeping through your life; whether you see them or not doesn't matter. Toast your new home, toast the fun travel, and toast the best friends who are able to join you; toast the "work" (dance-with-life) opportunities that now abound. Toast whatever it is you want as if you already had it. Celebrate real things, birthdays, rainbows, tooth fairies, and celebrate things of the future as if you were living there now, with your every cup, bowl, and tub overflowing.

Taking It to the Bank

In an illusionary world, custom-made for its inhabitants, by its inhabitants, who have the power to change all things no matter where they've been, there's "enough" material and ethereal abundance for everyone. Experiencing it, owning it, creating it, is relatively easy—just look at the people who've done so. You are Divine Intelligence experiencing your choice to fleetingly believe in the lies of here versus there, now versus then, and have versus have-not, because you can, because it's fun, and to see what may come of it based upon your own sense of adventure. You possess default settings to naturally achieve whatever you wish for. Money is the least you can manifest. For your mere presence upon earth, in this hallowed realm of which you are king, you can have anything you want once you know how to get it.

CHAPTER 8

WHAT YOU REALLY WANT

If I feel happy with things as they now are, aren't I settling for less than what I really want?

Is having "desires" the problem?

Which is better?

To be happy and poor, or to be rich and bored?

Is there a different choice?

How do we live in the "now" without giving up on our dreams?

The happiest?

Happier?

How can I be happy?

I think there's more.

Is that all?

Does anyone really know what they really want?

If material things are merely props, and my success at amassing them by following these ideas is so inevitable, the whole chase seems pretty shallow. So, what comes later? Can I go straight there instead? Is there something I can aim for now that is more meaningful? What is it I really want?

You know what you want, but you ask anyway, as if it were the eternal "unknowable." *You want to be happy.* It's the best part of every adventure, it's why you want to live, to thrive, to heal, and to love. The reason you want each of these is: to be happy. It's the ultimate end result, happiness. Any and every other desire, besides happiness, exists so that you will be happy, which means that anything you want other than happiness is a "cursed how" on the way to happiness, so why not just start there, with happiness as your stated end result? Which is indeed your question.

The answer is: because you've been taught otherwise. Taught that you must figure out how you'll get there. People usually prefer to name goals like losing weight, paying off debt, finding their "soul mate," or coming into a fortune, and because they want these things so ferociously, they ultimately forget the reason why . . . their happiness. To most people, happiness without these things, well, that's just happiness, and who wants to be happy when you have challenges and unrealized dreams? To most, happiness, in this moment, implies settling for less or merely making the best of what they have. What a colossal misunderstanding! Why? Because they've not yet grasped that happiness *also* offers a fast track to paying off debt, losing weight, finding the "soul mate," coming into the fortune, and all else, material and spiritual.

In truth, given today's rampant misunderstandings of all things pertaining to life on earth, to finally insist upon and strive for a new definition of happiness, followed with behavior in alignment with it, offers the ultimate life Reset button. It's grease for the wheels of the Universe, which can then spin in your favor, drawing to you whatever your heart desires. Happiness isn't a crop you harvest when your dreams come true, it's the fertilizer that makes them come true faster. It's not the destination, but the path. Not something to put off, but to put on. Not tomorrow, but right now. To be clear, we're not talking about you tiptoeing through tulips for the rest of your life, dancing nonstop, laughing hysterically, or smiling from ear to ear as you go about wearing rose-colored glasses.

We're talking about you living your bliss, and doing so by actively facing your fears, dealing with your challenges, putting out your fires, taking action even when you're lost, and thereby becoming more than you now know is possible. We're talking about a life well lived, that will, of course, naturally include time off for rest, play, and spontaneity. This is the recipe for true happiness.

This isn't new, everyone knows life is about happiness . . .

Everybody thinks they know what happiness is, yet based upon most people's choices, it's quite evidently the one thing they know the least about. Unfortunately, however, because you think you already know what it means, the conversation ended a long time ago.

People prefer to externalize the reasons for their happiness. Otherwise they'd have to see themselves as responsible for it.

Even today, with hearts and minds opening at this new dawn in time, people still don't realize that happiness lies right beneath their nose; that happiness is not something to attain or earn, it's something you choose. People want to believe that emotions, including happiness, happen to you. That they are a natural, predictable function of life happening to you. They think their prevailing mood is what anyone would feel if anyone had to endure what they have had to endure. As if some days or months or years life just happens to work out, and so you are just happy, and others not so much, and you just feel depressed, that you're otherwise helpless to change these moods. Where, in truth, every second of every day, contrary to appearances, you can choose joy, or not. It was never "supposed" to be conditional.

As is debatably credited to a beloved, dead American president: *"Most folks are about as happy as they make up their minds to be"* (Abraham Lincoln).

And you know, in normal circles of people (you are so not normal), when Lincoln's words are shared, there's usually a gentle chuckle. Which proves the point, eh? If you were to say, "The sun rises every morning," that would not get a chuckle, right? Because it's the absolute truth that you build your lives around. If I were to say (to you), "Divinity dwells within all," that would not get a chuckle. But when you say, "Most people are about as happy as they make up their minds to be," it's viewed as light humor *because while all sense its truth, they themselves haven't "made up their minds"! Have you? See.*

People prefer to externalize the reasons for their happiness; it's much "safer." Otherwise they'd have to see themselves as responsible for it. Yet if you at least begin to ask some new questions and dig for new answers, you can quickly begin to grasp that just as you can choose perspectives that will yield anger, guilt, excitement, or fear, so must this be true of happiness. That no matter what may be going on in your life, you can choose perspectives that will be optimistic, favorable, loving, accepting, and ultimately happy. You'll see that not only is this now an option, but it's been why you've ever felt any emotion in the past. And if this is the case, so must it be true in this moment. Which means that if now, today, you are not feeling happy, it's always because of choices you're making that can now be revisited.

Going a step further, again, galling as this is to read, the idea of free will and choice being the cornerstone of your emotions means that whatever you've felt in the past, it was what you most *wanted* to feel. Maybe not consciously, maybe not directly, yet clearly, as the indisputable fountainhead of your emotions, yourself, not other people or circumstances, to feel anything means you *chose* to feel it over all other feelings. Yeah, even depression is a choice in this light. This is huge because it puts you in the driver's seat, albeit very hard to believe at first. Hypothetically, this may lead to indignation, "I just lost my job. I've got credit card bills. I was molested as a kid. I'm going to lose my house. And you're telling me I want to be depressed?" Yes. Are you telling me you are powerless? Would you rather choose proud, giddy, and excited? You'd probably feel a bit silly if you couldn't stop smiling. "You're telling me I want to be unhappy when someone's broken my heart?" Yes. You could choose happy; however, sadness would actually *feel better* than happiness, under the circumstances. Always you choose, directly or indirectly. And by seeing this, you finally realize you can choose otherwise, and your power begins to return.

It's safe for many people not to be happy, otherwise their lightheartedness may give the appearance that they're OK with any disappointments in their life. By being depressed, heartbroken, jealous, regretful, unhappy, it's as if you're saying to others, "Please, this is so not my choice! I'm powerless to these awful circumstances and crazy people! I'm vulnerable! Can you blame me? I'd be so much more successful if it weren't for all these idiots. This is what I have to deal with!"

I don't agree! Most people are fully prepared to accept responsibility for their happiness. At least I am.

Yes, but are you as prepared to accept full responsibility for your every twinge of *un*happiness?

Right. "*That's* usually someone else's fault!"

Not anymore.

Happiness as the ultimate end result simultaneously becomes the ultimate responsibility—yours. One hundred percent. And should you wake up to this truth, which is the choice your world is now faced with in the evolution of consciousness, you'll realize that just as you can't blame someone else for what's happening in your life, neither can you blame them for how you feel about it.

Are you up to that?

There's no more important thing to understand in the entire Universe, nor in your entire life, than your happiness. Happiness is the reason for everything, *everything*. Why do people want to lose weight, improve their health, or live pain-free but to be happy? Why do people want more money, more friends, more laughter? The car, the career, the vacations, the house, and a family are all sought for one reason: happiness. *Your own happiness.*

Even if you believe you care more about seeing loved ones happy . . . *haven't you* just named *your motivation* as being *what you most care about*? Divinely selfish, rock on. You have to, need to, must seek your own happiness, whether in the guise of selfishness or selflessness.

There's nothing you've ever done in your entire life that wasn't geared toward *your* happiness. It's not only the ultimate end result, but the ultimate inevitable. Basically, you have no choice. Renouncing it does you no good, for even the renunciation is your attempt to be happy. Doesn't matter that you don't name it or even see it. Even when you don't choose happiness, you are therefore choosing it.

Some might argue that life is all about love. Yet if you remember when we compared happiness to love, we saw that love is a constant. That "your lives are not about love, they are about adventures *into love*." Your adventures are the variable, and each adventure is led by your quest for joy. And your greatest revelation will come on the day you realize that happiness is not found, but chosen, and then, within it, you can move in ever-widening circles to encompass more and more of it, live your life with greater ease, as all things shall be added unto you.

I thought you said we are here for the adventure of it? But now it's happiness?

We could play with words, and it may again seem like we are, but in this type of dialogue, words are all we have, and they're enough. The reason you choose to go on spiritual adventures into time and space, just like taking vacations in your mortal life, is for the potential they contain for happiness, joy, or fun—using these words interchangeably. Yet as your adventures in romance, health, or abundance go, for example, you now erroneously tend to think that your happiness ought to be contingent on their outcome falling within a certain desired range, which simply does not need to be the case. Imagine a child going to a favorite theme park—what a great adventure! Isn't just being there reason to celebrate and feel joy? However, if they thought they had to ride every ride, sit at the front of each car or train, and meet every costumed character, it would turn into a chore, and even if they achieved everything they wanted, it would be far less fun than if they had viewed every moment as a gift. Not that "viewing every moment as a gift" would mean sitting in stillness at the theme park, learning to solemnly sense some deep inner appreciation—*yuck!* They'd still run around, whoop and holler, stand in lines, take some rides twice, plan *and* be spontaneous—cool! Do you see? The idea of a child not being happy at the park until endless tasks are completed—that's how you approach happiness in your life on earth. You and almost everyone else. It's time to start whooping and hollering a bit more, even as you run to the next ride.

What you have to discover is that you can be happy even as you create a life that gives you more to celebrate. Why not have your adventures into career, love, and money, and be happy in the process of their creation? Why not drop the idea that the ultimate reward depends upon outcomes, or upon some kind of penance, sacrifice, or suffering?

Suddenly, happiness appears beneath your very nose. Its attainment has only ever been a matter of focus and perception. It's been there all along for you to choose. You just have to want *it* more than you want to be *unhappy*, which is asking a lot from some people.

Consider, no matter what else you may ever achieve, conquer, or overcome during the rest of this lifetime, none of it will ever compare to the fact that you are even present in your hallowed jungles of time and space. It's as if you and everyone else have *already* hit life's jackpot! You've already won the lottery for the life of your wildest dreams, but instead of checking your tickets, you all keep buying more!

You *can* choose to see yourself as the winner you already are, today. And once you do, something stunning happens. Your thoughts become things, *faster*. And your manifestations will come in ways where *more joy* will be added unto you. For example, one of the ways pure happiness manifests, in addition to whatever "things" have been thought about (if any), is through the "attraction" of new friends and bright ideas, soaring creativity, renewed self-confidence, inspired action or courage, as well as cool "stuff"— to any degree that such matters to you and is thus required if you are to experience the happiness you put forth.

So, being happy will ultimately make me happier?

Exactly! Like attracts like. Your happiness will not only mean more joy in the present moment, but it will literally jockey the players and circumstances of your life, known and unknown, just as your thoughts do, predisposing you to so-called accidents, coincidences, and serendipities that will yield all things, tangible and intangible, that will perpetuate and replicate conditions and manifestations for *more* happiness. It all starts happening faster and faster, because when you're happy, you resist less, play more, worry less, try harder, show up, take action, dream bigger, and thereby allow for maximum, high-speed transformation.

Don't think there's something wrong with you because you want things that you don't yet have.

Can I have another cheat sheet? Maybe "21 Steps on How to Choose Happiness" this time?

Happiness is easier than amassing a fortune, not that either are difficult. This time, you'll need only six steps to help you choose happiness now:

1. DROP THE CONTINGENCIES

Not giving yourself permission to be happy is a showstopper. Three common contingencies that get in the way of happiness-now are: waiting to hit the big home run, waiting to feel more "complete," and waiting to feel more worthy.

Permission Contingent on Hitting the BIG Home Run

A great secret to living the life of your dreams is to start living them, today, to any degree you can. Maybe you can't afford to vacation in Tahiti; can you afford Tampa? Maybe you haven't found your "twin flame" to travel with; can you go alone or with a best friend? Maybe you'll actually meet your "twin flame" . . . *in Tampa.* Do not wait for "all" by choosing nothing or you'll likely wait for the rest of your life. Partial enjoyment is not only fun but heightens the expectation of greater successes in the future, making these seem more attainable and believable.

Postponing not only dampens all of your senses, it leads to a greater sense of helplessness, only further discouraging you. Again, like attracts like. This time it will push you into a state of overwhelm since nothing on your dream radar is matching up with reality, paralyzing you at a time when action is most needed. "I dream of a champagne-and-caviar lifestyle, I'm *not about* to accept a job working for some low hourly pay!"

Your action steps today and tomorrow do not define who you are. They're just steps. Choosing "nothing" instead of something may literally shut down your awesome life. See your baby steps as baby steps, not as compromised dreams.

Permission Contingent on Feeling Complete

Don't think there's something wrong with you because you want things that you don't yet have. And don't, therefore, put your happiness off until you do have those things.

Remember the *Divine Sense of Incompletion*? Evidence of the presence of greatness within you? Proof divine consciousness is present? A consciousness, by definition, that yearns to expand eternally? Which means it always exists in a state of wanting "things" it does not yet have? It's among your greatest gifts that will ensure you are always in motion. Wanting stuff that you don't yet have doesn't mean something's wrong with you, it means that everything is right, you are where you should be, and God dwells within! Most importantly, it means you have every reason to be happy *right now.*

You will, of course, as shared earlier, eventually manifest everything you now desire, but in those moments of attainment, you'll see farther, know more, and discover you could have asked for even "better, faster, or funner," and new desires will be born. If you are postponing your happiness until you feel complete, neither happiness nor completeness will ever come to pass. Instead, choose both: be happy with who you already are, all you've already done, the miracles of life itself, while simultaneously striving to become "more" each and every day.

Permission Contingent on Feeling Worthy

Finally, there are folks who put off their happiness because they're not yet feeling worthy. They criticize and berate themselves because they think they're too lazy, they've got too much clutter, they just don't have what it takes to focus properly, they feel undisciplined, they sleep too much, eat too much, or watch TV too much, and so on.

Have you considered, however, that it just might be your downtime, your lounging-in-bed-too-long time, your walkabout time, watching-the-rain time, and your sad-and-lonely times that are exactly what will make possible your highest achievements and greatest joys? What if they were the *necessary* moments of rest and contextualization that greatness demanded? Would they still make you feel guilty? Or might you allow yourself to enjoy them?

Ease up on yourself. See the ebb and flow, balance and perfection, in all things, especially your life on earth. This is not the world you think it is, you are not being judged, you are not supposed to be some idealized vision of perfection. You have never let anyone down. Nothing is expected. This is your game, and you get to live by your imagined, magical rules.

2. CHOOSE IT

Do you have to work?
Do you have to chauffeur kids around town?
Do you have to exercise?
Do you have to budget your money, energy, and time?
Do you have to watch what you eat?
Or . . . do you have the extraordinary, fleeting privilege of *getting* to do these things?

To state the obvious, there are people right now who would very much like to work, but they can't get a job. Who want kids but for any number of reasons can't have them. Who would love the kinds of problems that come with having money, a busy social calendar, or a modicum of free time.

There are people right now, the world over, who would "die" to have your life.

You *get* to eat? How many times a day?!

Life is an exercise in perspectives, all of which are chosen. Choose to see the good, the fair, the beauty, the grace, the Divine, and you will forever be adding to the body of evidence and reasons you already have to also choose "happy."

3. GRATITUDE AND APPRECIATION

Gratitude and appreciation, like all thoughts and feelings, attract similar thoughts and, ultimately, circumstances, which manifest those feelings within you all over again. This is the perpetuation and replication of the scenario we just saw for happiness. Like all thoughts, gratitude and appreciation rearrange your life so that you will have more reasons to be grateful and appreciative.

Authentic gratitude and appreciation, verbally or silently *feeling* "thank you," are tantamount to saying, "I have received." And accordingly, in a world where your thoughts and words become things, the only way "I have received" can be actualized is if you do, later, receive. This is what those words, not necessarily spoken, will spark, combined with all else we've been discussing, including visualizing, baby steps, and acting "as if." By putting these feelings out there for what you have already received, you will receive more of the same, and *by putting them out there for what you have not yet received, but as if you had, you will*, and your reasons to be happy shall increase.

Concerning "all else we've been discussing," even though gratitude and appreciation are feelings, by now it should be clear that if you want change, you must physically act. It is the cherry on top of being congruent and in full resonance with the vision you now hold for changes you wish to manifest.

Picture in your mind a person in a fancy living room recliner, day in and day out, watching TV and eating donuts. If this person suddenly turned to you and said, "What a beautiful day. I feel so blessed. I truly appreciate my life and therefore I'm excited about the great changes that are now barreling down upon me!" You'd be like, "What life? Are you serious?" But they continue, "I so appreciate the gifts 'God' has given me." You'd seriously wonder what they're talking about. "All you do is watch TV and eat donuts." Right? Indignant? Not that someone couldn't enjoy all their time eating donuts in front of the TV, but if they are going on about their life being transformed, something isn't lining up.

This is not the world you think it is, you are not being judged, you are not supposed to be some idealized vision of perfection.

Similarly, true gratitude and appreciation would always entail, to whatever actual or pretend degree possible, a proper utilization and indulgence in that which it is expressed for. If you live in the United States, can you really feel emotional gratitude and appreciation for rain now falling over a parched town in Mongolia? For a new species of frog found in Tasmania? For stunning geological formations just discovered on the moon? Is there any emotional connection? Similarly, to give thanks for your blossoming abundance, health, and friendships, while making no physical demonstrations, means you're not emotionally feeling it.

Don't give gratitude and appreciation mere lip service. The best way you can really get into such modes is through utilizing what little you may have, from where you are, seizing the day, taking action, going out more, enjoying whatever gifts you have (and you *do* have gifts), and enjoying the miracles of life.

4. DIE TO THE ILLUSIONS

The ultimate "test" to living in the jungles of time and space, again pertaining to its greatest hook and in large part the reason you're there, is learning to move with your dreams, even as they are contradicted, 24/7, by the illusions of time, space, and matter. Thinking, speaking, and behaving as if your desired vision for the future was more real than earlier manifestations that still surround you, even as you have to consider and live among them each day. You're an infinite being now voluntarily "trapped" in an illusionary world that your physical senses tell you is *real*. Yet thinking so means you also believe that you are small, ineffective, and unimportant. You can beat this. You know life rocks and you're important. You wouldn't have played along if you couldn't ultimately make sense of this and uncover the truth amid a world of lies.

You are hereby tasked with seeing through, dying to, the illusions, learning of your supremacy over them! You are to refrain from committing the original sin, eating the forbidden fruit every single day, which was biting into the *illusion* of an apple, and all other illusions, thinking it and they were real. Not that the illusions should be *entirely* transcended, obliterated, let's walk on water—we already covered that. This was *not* the goal. Doing so would defeat the reason you're here, to adventure *within* the illusions. But to get your groove on and have as much fun as possible, you can and will see them in their proper context—as stage props that you have dominion over, not a reality that has dominion over you!

For example, using your physical senses you can assess today's economy and surmise, "Oh, my chances of living in more wealth this year don't look so good. Trends are declining. Consumption is flat. And most indexes are showing this will persist for some time." Or you can now choose to go within, grounded in truth, and understand that there's almost no connection to what's happening in the illusions to your ability to manifest wealth. Every single day, even now, the world over, first time millionaires are made. *Today*, no doubt, within 100 miles of where you're reading this, someone is being added to the list. No biggie. See the obvious. Die to the illusions and be born again to truth. This is what was meant by that biblical adage. It was not meant to be interpreted as "be born again to some man-made religious ideology," but be born, again, as who you *really* are, a spiritual being who creates your own reality with the focus of your attention through thought, word, and action.

And so now you're living the choice you made to be here, and if you want to begin remembering who you really are, to live as happily as you know you can be, you're then ready to wake up to these greater ideas, steady and determined, and die to the illusions you once thought represented reality.

5. VISUALIZE HAPPINESS

Most often, creative visualization is used for getting a new car, house, or relationship, but it works for more happiness too, which, as noted, can also accelerate the arrival of a new car, house, or relationship, without you even thinking of those things. For all of the reasons already given when talking about gratitude and appreciation, visualizing more happiness will beget more happiness.

Try this: instead of visualizing *things* you feel joy over, just visualize joy. Smile wide across your face, laughing, high-fiving friends, receiving congratulations, pats on the back, and slow-motion fist bumps, with a sense of delirium and celebration. Days, weeks, or months later, such joy will be made manifest by bringing with it exactly the right people, toys, confidence, inspiration, and circumstances necessary for you to authentically feel it—even though you thought not of these things. In this case, they would be the earlier-discussed "unexpected manifestations" that were drawn into your life as the means for making you as happy as you had earlier imagined, the "unthought-of" territory.

In the instant you decide you're ready to remember who you really are, to demonstrate your beliefs, and to live out loud, your entire inheritance will be restored.

6. BE GENTLE WITH YOURSELF

The last point for getting your happiness on is to be gentle with yourself. In an instant-gratification society, you too quickly turn against yourself when you feel impatient with change. Labeling yourself, blaming yourself, putting yourself into a tiny little box of condemnation, all of which further removes you from being happy and, worse, attracts more ideas of your feared inadequacies. Be kind to yourself. You're doing your very best, always have. You're going to get it right, and faster when you relax.

Like the prodigal son in the Bible, the one who turned his back on his father's wealth, only to come home broke, upon which his jubilant father restored his entire inheritance—you are that son, metaphorically speaking. Beguiled by the stunning and spectacular illusions of this gorgeous illusionary world, you turned your back on the truth of your source and heritage. And "falling from grace," you slipped, got hurt, and convinced yourself that you were mere mortal. Enough already. Your father, metaphor for *the truth,* patiently awaits your return. You're not any less for your follies and foibles, but more. Your departure wasn't a mistake, it was *courageous.* Your return to grace is inevitable. Even today, half asleep in ignorance, you're adored as much as you ever had been. And in the *instant* you decide you're ready to remember who you really are, to demonstrate your beliefs, and to live out loud, your entire inheritance will be restored.

The Most Powerful Change Agent in Time and Space

If you haven't gathered by now, let me tell you one of the very coolest things about making happiness your end result:

It implies, and therefore forces, all things necessary for your happiness to fantastically come into your life.

Meaning, from this day forward, with happiness as your guiding light, you are off the hook as Micromanager of the Universe. Even big things, hugs and stuff, will be drawn to you. All you have to do is think, speak, and *act* on your happiness, and all that's necessary for *you* to be *that* happy will be added.

Right? Logical? If you are imagining and feeling great joy, and taking action on it, the only way it can find and authentically possess you is if all the cylinders are firing in your life on earth. You're not going to be authentically joyful if you're broke, right? Unemployed? Sick? Lonely? Confused? Unhealthy?

Like a boomerang, your thoughts and feelings leave you and go beyond the curtains of time and space, where they whirl and gather and collect, on a mission to come back into your life as soon as possible, as best friends, agents, travel partners, confidence, inspiration, and so much more, to make you feel all over again the thoughts and feelings that summoned them. So, if your end result is true, euphoric happiness, how can that happen in any other way than a total life transformation?

Moving toward great happiness, *with* great happiness, is not going to trick you into feeling it without justification. It is not going to merely twist your perceptions so you'll be happy for what you have and settle for less than what you want! It is not going to leave you jilted at the altar of love. None of these would bring happiness to anyone. Nor is it going to train you to live a hermit's life devoid of desire. Instead, it will lead you to your greatest discoveries, your highest heights, your deepest loves, your finest health, and your richest treasures. Revealing one of your reality's most questioned secrets: happiness is life's ultimate end result.

CHAPTER 9

Can We Talk?

How do we know and find out our purpose?

Can other people hold us back?

Why are some people seemingly able to remember past lives?

Does déjà vu come from knowing someone in a past life?

How can I know as much as you?

How do you explain the catastrophic accident that creates life-altering or life-ending conditions?

What comes "after" the time-space continuum?

I have to ask, are there aliens among us?

My uncle committed suicide— is he OK?

Your answers create more questions, about everything from aliens to angels to happiness—the first being, wouldn't the mind of God already know how this is all going to play out?

"Infinite" is not just theoretical. It means there are an unending, and therefore unknowable, number of ways something, including each lifetime, may unfold. Not even "God" knows what will happen next, even within a range of *infinite* probabilities, nor how your dreams will come true! You can, nevertheless, know that all will go well and that your dreams, when defined wisely, unencumbered with specific details, hows, or people, will come true. You can know that everyone will return "home" to truth. That you are safe, loved, and guided. And you can also know that you never actually "went" anywhere.

Are we like a dumbed-down version of God?

That you're even having this conversation, inside the dream, *while dreaming*, having figured this much out, shows you are anything but dumb.

Is it an accident that some people remember prior lives, or can we all do it deliberately?

All can develop their ability to recall, and many have already done just that. But the most important thing for anybody to consider is their present lifetime. If you were born remembering all of your lives, it could really clutter things up—particularly given how immature you presently are as a society, believing in faulting others for your unpleasant manifestations, victimhood, and the rest. Can you imagine lawsuits stemming from grievances in past lives? "He chopped my head off during the Inquisition!"

For now, it's as much intentional as it is unintentional that you don't remember.

I am constantly reminded that I have a purpose in being here. What if I don't know what that purpose is, or what if I feel like I've already achieved that purpose? Am I wasting my time?

If you're breathing, you're now filling that one sacred, special niche that no one else could ever fill. Your eyes see what no others will ever see, your ears hear what no others will ever hear, and your perspective and feelings will never, ever be duplicated. Without you, the Universe would be less.

This is your highest offering. Being "you" is a sacred role that no one else could ever fill. And so if you're here, you're doing it. Your "purpose" has no more to do with your profession or calling than the color of your socks or what you had for breakfast. It's not what you do or don't do, whether you love it or hate it or change it a hundred times. As long as you're here, you're filling that niche—being who no one else has *ever* been.

You cannot be "the whole show"—or
the only game in town.

Thinking otherwise puts you in that false mind-set of, "If there is one thing I'm *supposed* to be doing, that means that everything else I'm doing is *wrong!* There's a reason I'm here, and I need to find out what it is because until I do, everything else is just a 'dishonest' waste of time." Too much pressure and for no reason, as it's completely untrue.

So do what makes you happiest, or at least what you think might ultimately make you happiest. Follow your heart, and if your heart isn't leading you anywhere, then wherever you are right now is likely where you have the most to learn. These considerations will ultimately increase both your reach and impact on the world, not that you have to do either.

I have to ask, are there aliens among us?

Of course there are! Not just in the stars, but upon the earth, too.

First, assessing the brilliance of the physical universe, even with physical senses alone, and grasping the immense intelligence that had to be involved in bringing it into being, it becomes *impossible* to conclude that a piddly few billion humanoids happen to represent the totality of conscious co-creators within it. *Impossible.* This would be like you finding an ancient Roman coin on a Mediterranean beach and wondering if it was the only Roman coin ever minted. Or wondering if the real reason Divine Intelligence created the cosmos was to roast marshmallows.

That you are even here, which alone should be *utterly* impossible, indicates something colossal is going on, something of an intelligence, grace, and love that is truly inconceivable. You are of it, but shockingly small compared to it, and thus, you cannot be "the whole show"—or the only game in town.

Second, the normal presumption when humans ask about the existence of extraterrestrials is that they're physical beings, about your shape and size. Why would that be true? Some are, but others live in an ethereal, nontangible state. Some share your space but are invisible to your physical senses. Some are visible but have shifted their shapes to blend in.

Can we trust them?

Most, especially the ones that visit you, have far superior technology to yours, which is a by-product of their own earlier spiritual awakening, and, clearly, if they wanted to hurt you, they would have by now. Which is not to say they aren't still learning and making mistakes. Incidentally, if and when you meet them, your behavior must still be guided by your own heart and mind, not what you read here or anywhere else. Only you know what's best for you.

Human civilization will not have the mind-numbing breakthroughs in the sciences necessary to match their technologies, without first having a blossoming awareness of its true spiritual nature, grasping that all are love beings, of a divine, eternal nature. So far, the more technologically advanced *you've* become, the more polluted the planet has gotten and the bigger a mess you've made. But humanity is still in its absolute infancy compared to jumping around from one galaxy to the next. You're stuck in a loop where time and again, whether it was the Greeks, the Romans, the Egyptians, or the Atlanteans, you've excelled technologically at a much faster rate than spiritually, leading to decline and oblivion.

Extraterrestrials who can planet-hop, who seem to defy all the physical laws that you know, have first developed themselves as more awakened beings, incorporating and mingling their knowledge of consciousness, science, and the physical universe, to harness energies and laws that are otherwise unattainable. Accordingly, given their spirituality and related ethics, the *last thing* they'd ever want to do is barbarically plunder your earth and people, steal your minerals, or eat your flesh.

Instead, for now, most have chosen only to send out scouts who are under the strictest of guidelines, like your conservationists who visit the Maasai Mara, to "leave things exactly as they find them," for to do otherwise, to get involved, to impose laws or point out follies, may interfere with your own free will and spiritual evolution.

What is déjà vu? Do these feelings come from memories and comfort levels attained in a past life?

Sometimes.

Perhaps, in a past life, you were in places or with people that you are now revisiting, thus making them feel oddly familiar, even though in this lifetime, you are meeting "them" for the first time. Or maybe in a nighttime dream or other altered state, you literally scouted out the people and places that you would likely be meeting in certain probable tomorrows, creating the familiarity.

The main thing to consider when these esoteric ideas are being weighed is that, for the most part, *it doesn't matter why you feel déjà vu*. What matters is what you choose, today. Too often people draw false and limiting conclusions when they jump ahead of themselves and try to nail down all of their feelings. "Wow, this is so strong, it must be destiny, meant to be." Nothing is meant to be! And then they try to channel their energy into a relationship or a business that sparked the feeling, thinking that "it's supposed to work." Nothing is "supposed" to work! You get to decide. You get to try out new ideas, friendships, or adventures. Whether or not you knew someone in a past life, or just met them for the first time in all of your lives, does not change how important they could potentially be to you now. To think that every sensed feeling of déjà vu must have deep meaning and must be given a high priority could limit you from exploring other exciting options that may also lie on your horizon.

Are we limited by the thoughts of others or of the public?

Yes, but only to the *minimal* degree that you agreed to be limited when you chose this lifetime on your planet, under the prevailing, well-known conditions. *But never to the degree that they could keep you from knowing peace, love, abundance, health, and joy today.*

If we are eternal beings, what happens to those who commit suicide? If "nothing matters," life is just an illusion, and we all have super-cool friends waiting for us on the other side, is suicide OK?

True, you will live forever and ever. And if you want, after this lifetime, you can come back 500,000 more times and still have *eternity* before you. But understand, too, that there is not one instant in any of your future incarnations that will replicate exactly the potential, probabilities, gifts, and opportunities that now, today, exist for your adventures, your advancement, your comeback, your evolution, your glory, and your happiness. When you come back, you won't have what you have now. Life goes on and on and on and on, but you being who you are today, with the gorgeous opportunities and the chosen challenges now before you, will never come again.

True, you will live forever and ever.

The people you now love and the people who you might still love, as well as the ways you love them, will never be just as they are today. They'll be back, but playing a different role, wearing a different hat, under different pretenses. What you have today can never be duplicated.

However great the emotional pains you may feel in this lifetime, the euphoria of facing them and moving beyond them will be far greater. There is order; just because you can't see it doesn't mean it's not there. Get up, go out, hang in there. Be among people. Do your best.

Life is precious, yours is irreplaceable, and you are important. Besides, *you're going to die anyway.* Whether it's 10 days from now or 100 years from now. Your days are already numbered. And since this is going to happen anyway, and since your mere presence in the illusions reflects a deeper greater will to be here, it would never be wise (with a few extreme exceptions) to contradict your own higher self's choice.

Furthermore, as a forever being, do you really think if you die now, shaving, hypothetically, 30 years off your natural life through suicide, you will have accomplished much in the scheme of eternity—other than wreaking havoc in the lives of those you most love and who love you the most? Or is it revenge you are likely after? Revenge through suicide is, as you say, "cutting off your nose to spite your face." First, because those you aim to hurt will get over your deed while concluding you were a little "off," if they're even that kind. Second, after the "act," you'll still be faced with the confusion and pain that led you to take your life, combined with a deep sadness for the emotional carnage you will have wrought upon those survivors who did, in fact, love you, magnified by your sheer inability to reach out to them. Last, you will soon be shown that the thinking of yours that created the confusion and pain must still be sorted out, and the best way to do this is to meet those thoughts, as things, in a brand-new incarnation.

Conversely, if you "tough things out" over the course of your remaining life, first, you will naturally have rebounded so far and high, you won't even believe you were ever suicidal, and second, you're going to think to yourself, "Dang, that was so *fast*. I'm 94 already? So fast! What an awesome life I had, hardships and all."

If 1,000 years ago the world population was under two billion, and now it's like six or seven billion, where did all these people or souls come from?

First, why would all people/souls have to be on earth at the same time? Couldn't they have time off in between lifetimes? And haven't we covered that there *are* other realms and dimensions that conscious creators exist in, rather than only Earth?

Second, don't you think there are probably other planets inhabited by humans or at least humanoids that could also be occupied by any of you?

Third, how about the alternate and parallel universes that are rumored to exist? Couldn't they also be home to people/souls who were not on the earth when counts were much lower?

If we live and exist for eternity, how are there baby souls?

Depends on perspective. From "outside" of the illusions, words like *baby* fail. But from "within" they're a useful "handle" on the experience. Just as you now understand that time is an illusion, you still experience your life linearly, seeming to progress from being a baby into older age. Similarly, from "within" the illusions, there will still be a "first" lifetime and a "last."

My friend Angela wants me to ask for your take on romantic relationships. WHY ARE THEY SO HARD? What is the whole point?

Please tell Angela that you characterize the past and the future based on your feelings today, so even though you now feel they have always been hard, this is more likely a characterization of what you're now going through than what life has actually shown you. Further, as your thoughts become things, those "observations" (creations) that are not pleasing you should not, ideally, be given such lip service, without running the risk of perpetuating that which is unpleasant.

If you don't like what you're seeing or how you're now feeling, you can change it by using all else we've been talking about, and by changing it, you'll start bringing about a different experience. Don't be lulled into the trap of thinking, "the way things are today is the way they're going to be tomorrow." Today has very little to do with the way things will be tomorrow.

Moreover, as shared earlier, if you're struggling in a relationship or with money or with creating a more fulfilling life, consider it a gift. It means something has been brought to your attention, something within you needs attention, and until the gift arrived, you didn't even know it. You have buttons being pressed that you would not know existed if you weren't feeling what you're now feeling.

This doesn't mean you have to stay in a relationship or situation that isn't pleasing you, but sometimes part of the attraction to someone is exactly to have your buttons pressed. Have an open mind and see if you can't use it to identify and eradicate limiting beliefs so that you can become a better, greater, or stronger person.

In or outside of your relationships, be happy. Your life is not about the other person. They do not define you. If you can shine right now, if you can live a well-rounded life, taking action, on the go, beaming and glowing in every area of your life—at work, at home, with family, following passions and interests—everybody is "gonna want some of dat."

I'm often asked by others why it's easier for them to believe the bad and how they can change this.

This question is based on a false premise. It takes for granted that *it is* easier to believe in the bad. You are all so much more positive and creative and optimistic than you give yourselves credit for. Every day you apply yourself, right? You show up, right? You prepare, right? You think, right? You imagine, right? You try, right? All of which shows that an eternal optimist dwells within, alive and well, and if you are honest, it usually prevails. This is your nature! It's how you've been so outrageously successful as a people.

Like the answer to the previous question, when you get poked and you frown at yourself, it feels like you're always failing, but you're not seeing all that's so right and so strong and so present in yourself that also exists in that moment. Yet, if you don't see it and you keep thinking poorly of yourself and you keep believing that that question could even be real, you lower your energy to the point where you feel powerless, and the shadow it casts can seem to consume all else.

Don't buy it. You're allowed to have a bad day, bad month, bad however-long-it-takes. It won't be who you are. It's fleeting. Just a step on the path, not the path itself. Look at your track record. Look at the adversity you've already been through. The times you've been knocked down and got back up. The times you were lost but found yourself. And if you go through a dark spell ever again, it's not because you're negative. It's not because you're bad. Soon the sun will rise, the gloom will suddenly seem like a distant memory, and you'll wonder how you ever could have let so little feel like so much.

Parents in my audiences always ask me what's the best thing they can do to help their children understand this stuff. Now that I have a child, I'd love to read your answer.

Be the example. That you even asked that question, you know enough to do enough to be the best you can be. Of course, talk to them. Tell them to pick their chin up if they're feeling down. Show them the bright side of things. Teach them that their thoughts become things. When they feel bad, they should try to understand why and not ignore their feelings. Surround them in the truth. Get them little books. Lead them into the understanding of life that you now have by example and by instruction.

Are there "elite groups" at large in the world that supposedly have sway over politics and economies? Do they exist? Are we at their mercy?

It doesn't matter if they exist, because no matter what anybody else is doing in the world, no matter who is supposedly being manipulated, it doesn't take away from the fact that you are a divine, spiritual being, that you decide what's going to happen for the rest of your life, and no one can keep you from "yours" when it comes to happiness, love, friendship, creative, fulfilling work, and even money, in virtually any country.

You knew that you were choosing to be born into primitive times, spiritually speaking. You saw that you might pollute the world beyond recognition, that everyone would be throwing bombs at each other, that many would be poisoning their own bodies with chemicals and low-quality foods. You saw those possibilities existing on the stage you chose, for reasons that will one day make sense. But apart from cumulative mass decisions and politics, there still exists massive private individual freedom in each of your lives to be happy, that you needn't worry about the ill intentions of a very, very tiny few people.

As far as the economy, your wealth has less to do with what other people are experiencing, more to do with your thoughts, words, and actions. If you want more money, first imagine possessing it, and then physically move toward acquiring it, however seemingly futile. Mix things up. Get out more. Try stuff. And know that you're guided, protected, and loved.

How do we accept those in our lives for exactly who they are? How can we be less judgmental of them?

By not thinking that your own happiness somehow depends on what they think, say, and do.

You are untouchable by others, unless you allow them into your space. This seems to be anything but true, nevertheless, it is. Not understanding your safety among others, you start thinking that if your spouse or employer or best friend doesn't treat you with more respect or give you a raise, then you can't be all that you were meant to be, but this simply is not true and totally gives away your power.

First, everyone in your life was attracted to you by your thoughts, beliefs, and expectations. Second, you significantly influence their behavior toward you once they arrive. Third, with certain few exceptions, no matter how they behave, you can choose to learn and grow from it, and ultimately, to be happy in spite of them.

When you can be happy yourself without needing someone else's approval, without needing someone to behave a certain way, then not only are you free, but you free them from your own judgment.

Is our planet now overpopulated?

Physically, logistically, there's room for many more billions on earth. The challenge, however, is sustainability. The bigger question is not the number of people your planet can hold, but whether or not you can take care of yourselves academically, socially, and responsibility-wise, while not viewing each other as statistics, customers, and numbers.

Imagine, ideally, a small village or neighborhood, perhaps from an era gone by, in which everyone pretty much knew everyone, and everyone cared. Some in the village were farmers, some made clothing, some were teachers, some were lawyers, bankers, and accountants, etc. Imagine that every profession was represented in perfect balance. In such a village, if a neighbor fell terribly ill, you could rest assured that others would make it their priority to visit, to bring food, and to even help pay some bills until they were well again. Imagine another neighbor's child skipping school and getting into trouble. Everyone aware would want to help this child make better choices, speaking to parents, teachers, and the child herself. Can you see that such a community would be close, trusting, loving, nurturing, and supportive of its citizenry? Sure, boundaries would be everyone's concern, responsibility, and privilege. And of course, privacy would be respected, while at the same time there'd be a realization that "if any one of us hurts, we all hurt," and similarly, "when any one of us succeeds, loves, is loved, and lives happily, we all win."

Such a community would be able to handle any modest growth or shrinkage, but if there were demographic changes too great for people to be kept up with, suddenly, each stranger to you would be a depersonalized "neighbor," who probably plays his music too loud and lets his dog "mess" on your green lawn. Slowly but very surely, there would be a fraying of the society, disrespect, and a "me versus them" mentality. This, unfortunately, is where you now are in the world. Happily, you are more than powerful enough to see this yourselves and to correct it, because again, it's not the numbers that matter, but the degree to which you see each other as the brothers and sisters you are.

I now have a daughter, and I don't like that I worry about accidents. How do you explain the catastrophic accident that creates life-altering or life-ending conditions? How can I ward them off?

Any catastrophe, especially among the young, always *appears* random, chaotic, or like an accident.

Yet part of what you're learning, right now, is to rely less on your physical senses when interpreting reality, as if time and space were the starting point for all things. Your thoughts and your desires are the starting points, as are your daughter's, and the way they become the things, as we've been saying, is they literally rearrange the props on the stage of your life, choreographed with everyone else's other thoughts and relevant physical laws, until they find a point of entry. And such points of entry are invariably called, and appear to be, accidents, coincidences, serendipities, flukes, acts of God, and the like.

As you sense, she is safe from being an accidental statistic, and you need not fear that your normal, everyday precautions will bring about calamities. No more so than wearing a car seat belt yourself will attract you to accidents. Contrary to appearances, no adult or child has ever randomly suffered a catastrophic, life-altering accident *solely* because someone forgot to turn off a heater, left the screen door open to the pool, or forgot to cover electrical sockets.

Yet it is everyone's responsibility—which is perhaps the main topic we've been visiting throughout this journal—to care for and protect all they love and cherish, materially and spiritually. This would include diligence and consistency in creating a safe environment, of which turning off heaters, closing screen doors, and covering electrical sockets would be part. The loving intentions, followed up with the precautionary "baby steps," would help ensure, not guarantee, there would be no such events. Another part of the equation, however, is the love and intentions of all others involved, including infants, toddlers, and children. Not so much their conscious thoughts, which there may be no faculty for, but their greater selves and the lessons and adventures they have chosen.

Are you implying that before someone is born, they may choose their lifetime knowing it would end in a certain way, or that it would end "early"?

Every life is made up of *infinite probabilities* that are framed based upon who you are born to, when, social and political climates, your interests and curiosities, the interests of your parents, et cetera. Nothing is destined or predetermined, but many things are likely or probable. So, you could be well aware of certain probabilities that may unfold in a lifetime that you may be drawn to, including a possible early exit. Yet once any lifetime begins, probabilities shift, change, and evolve, and may or may not retain some of their earlier likelihoods. Ultimately, no matter what the starting point of a lifetime, decisions to exit can be made only at such time there is the option, never before. Still, yes, it is possible that a lifetime could be chosen with knowledge, or even a preference, that it might end "early" in a certain way.

When you said a child might live for a couple of years to be an example or to help heal, what about the flip side? What about the violator? Do they come in with a plan to violate others? Are they still treated the same way on the other side, as the "victim"?

No one is treated the same, but according to their thoughts and expectations, just like on earth. Further, there is no judgment and sentencing as you are otherwise taught.

Everyone means well. Everyone is of God. It's just that when some get really bent with confusion or fear—for instance, drawing the conclusion that if you want to get something done, you need to knock some heads, and if you don't, your head will be knocked—these are misunderstandings that can yield some hideous behavior. So, no one would choose a life to violate others, but this probability might exist very early in their life, based upon the degree of their confusion.

Just being there, alive, showing up for the fun of it, the Universe knows what you want, and "thy will shall be done."

Murderers are welcomed to the spiritual plane—loved and understood—while immediately, to the degree they're reachable, rehabilitation begins. This would generally start with them being shown how else they could have chosen to live, as well as *feeling* the pain of those they hurt and their survivors, and the repercussions upon the world for many generations.

You're living your lives in a massive dream bubble, and everybody's really a best friend to everybody else. Everybody is rooting for everyone else, and you're all doing your best, however misguided you may sometimes behave.

I've always been a goal setter, but can goals get in my way or become "cursed hows"?

Just being there, alive, showing up for the fun of it, the Universe knows what you want, and "thy will shall be done." If you're outside, living your life every day, moving with your heart, you will eventually and always have enough abundance, health, friends, confidence, creativity, etc., to live your bliss, on your terms, in your way.

Approach using goals on a case-by-case basis and reject the idea that they are mandatory. Use them if they empower or inspire you and not if they stress or seem to limit you.

Should our dreams be specific and detailed, or general and all-inclusive?

Dream, show up—boom. That's it. Doesn't matter if you get into details or remain general, however, there is a "Bermuda Triangle" of manifesting mistakes, which involves hazards related to attachment and insistence upon specificity, that you should be aware of:

1. attaching to unimportant details,

2. messing with the "cursed hows," and

3. insisting that specific people behave in certain ways.

You can automatically bypass these problem areas by having general end results. The snag, however, is that general end results don't usually excite you. To leap this hurdle, visualize the details that would likely come with the big general dream coming true, but be open to surprises. Don't insist on the details. Then there's not attachment, limitation, and stress. The details, in fact, are not what you're after, but you visualize them in this case to get yourself emotionally excited about the big picture of your life blasting off.

When people die do they become angels?

Not as you mean. There are different beings, or God-Particles like you, who just do that work. At death, however, there's no one pattern followed for what happens next. Some will go instantly on to other adventures in other realms, and others will linger for centuries and are often the cause of your ghost stories.

Additionally, after your passing, you can be in multiple places at one time, not that you can or should understand that now.

What right do I have to be happy in a sad world? What did I do to deserve so much? I never asked for this.

It's not a sad world. Not remotely. Some 99.99 percent of people polled would choose to keep living their life as opposed to losing it. Everyone, from the richest to the poorest, could make lists a thousand points long for why they love their life, as well as why they love life in general. And none of you would have a better list than any other.

And your good "fortune" is not about a "right" you have that others don't. Everyone creates their own reality, everyone has the same power, everyone is loved as much, everyone has their own reasons; it's just that you are judging them to be poor creators—they are not.

You may not have asked for this life, but you created it. And if others have not created what you are now enjoying, maybe it's because they already lived like you now live in their last 100 lifetimes, and today they're choosing to learn through new experiences, where perhaps the number of "things" in their life is of no importance. Experiences that *to you*, by your standards, based upon this lifetime alone, are unfavorable, yet experiences that they are enjoying.

This whole adventure of life in the jungles of time and space utterly takes your breath away. Even though it can sometimes be ugly and painful and nasty and disappointing, it nevertheless remains mind-blowing. And this is just as true for everyone else. Somehow, somewhere, in every single life, the number of things to be happy about wildly exceeds the number of things to be sad about.

Can you give me some concrete reasons or examples of reasons someone would choose to be born into poverty, illness, and famine?

More than we've already reviewed? Sure. But you realize you're implying they have nothing else in their lives other than poverty, illness, and famine. Fail. Why wouldn't they have mothers, fathers, brothers, sisters, friends, loves, hobbies, work, fulfillment, and dreams? Why wouldn't they savor the promise of each and every sunrise? Why wouldn't they also love butterflies and rainbows, chocolate and cupcakes, babies and singing and dancing? Salty oceans, warm sandy beaches, furry pets, foggy mornings, falling snow, desert sunsets, gurgling rivers, delicious food?

But this dialogue should be about you, remember? Stop looking to the "world out there" for answers about the "world in here." Solve *your* equations, find *your* happiness, and the world will prosper more than if you try to solve other people's equations and find their happiness.

OK, then, how else might you suggest I immediately begin enjoying my life more?

Accept where you are today. Be present. Have your dreams, but also master whatever's before you in the here and now. With such a shift, the pressure you've likely felt for the burden of living larger is gone, and you innately want to make the most of each day that remains, because *"Hot dog,* do days rock, or what?"

Acceptance does not mean settling for less. Don't worry that if you find enjoyment the way things are, you must somehow be lowering the bar on your ambitions, killing motivation, and negating your ability to create change. No such contradictions exist. Acceptance of what is and a roaring ambition for what might be are not mutually exclusive. In actuality, through acceptance, you stop resisting the present and you thereby clear the way for new and unexpected good things to reach you—given your divine propensity to succeed.

This works the same in personal relationships, which offer some of the most fertile grounds possible for learning, growing, and furthering your life's adventures. Unbeknownst to most, however, is how much energy they expend trying to change those who are in their life. Fearing that if they accept their partners, flaws and all, they'll be settling for less. Yet the happier you are, even if the reasons include overlooking their, or your, issues, the faster things will improve for you.

Which is not to say you can't also be working on improvements or even looking to make big changes; you just ought not do either to the degree it postpones your happiness in all that is already so wonderful.

Any other tips on being happy now, with things as they are, having no contingencies?

Actually . . . two more.

First, as you've gathered, humans are creatures of change. Nonstop, unending, forever change. Right?

And the desires beneath all hoped-for changes stem from mutually exclusive pros and cons. For example, strike it rich, and the unpaid bills go away. Or find your super-hot travel partner, and loneliness vanishes. You want change because there are either things you dislike about the present (the cons) or things you want about the future (the pros). And for every dislike, there is a corresponding like, and for every like, there is a corresponding dislike.

So, right now in your life, where you'd like change, these pros and cons exist. Right? Right. Which do you focus upon? The likes or the dislikes?

You're acing this.

Because of your thoughts becoming things *and* your inclination to succeed, not only is it more fun to think about the pros of change, but it brings such changes about faster because they're in alignment with your divine nature and your happy reasons for being alive.

Second, do you remember how, when you were a child, just the sight of a swing set or a pony or a Hula-Hoop would get your heart racing and your imagination somersaulting? That without even thinking in words, you felt that surely the world revolved around you, that you were the most special boy or girl ever to live, and that having fun was all that really mattered? (Actually, I still wonder how you knew so much at such a tender age.) The point being, give this to yourself again! You are me, choosing to be you. As far as you are concerned, there really is only you and I. What if everything and everyone else was of our imagination? Yes, trust me, this is closer to true than you can now fathom.

Acceptance of what is and a roaring ambition for
what might be are not mutually exclusive.

Honor yourself, cherish yourself, be yourself. And then, not only will you be pressed into the present moment, you'll be liberated from comparisons and judgments, from others and yourself. Suddenly, your little periscope on reality, placing you smack-dab at the center of your own life, will fill you with a sense of *being* enough, more than enough, everything. All else will appear as optional, far away, theoretical.

As a child, did you ever want candy tomorrow?! What's tomorrow, anyway? If there's fun to be had, right now is what matters.

With this new focus on you, in love, your own inner critic will be silenced by the majesty of the moment. What would be the point of looking elsewhere? And being centered in the present moment, all of your priorities will change. You'll see what's really important. You'll revel in wonder at the impossibility of creation. You'll feel lighter. Life will seem easier. Regrets evaporate, agendas vanish, and your innocence returns.

In a loving present moment, you will find:

- *The simplest of things can be the most miraculous.* If you had only seven more days to live, do you think you'd catch at least one sunrise? Yeah, probably all seven. And you'd be *awed* by each and every one. And similar splendors are everywhere, a cup of coffee or tea, a warm bed on a cold night, a cool bed on a hot night. Holding hands. The salt in the air at the beach. How *unbearably sweet* would these be if any or all were known to be among your "last ones"? And *everything* in your life can possess that kind of sweetness when you're in the now . . . *and you can put yourself there on purpose.*

- *There's more to life than achievement.* Although it's not to be underestimated for all that it promises in terms of adventure and learning, the other side of achievement when it's overvalued is that it's always linked to some unknown, ethereal future, pulling your attention away from the awesomeness of here and now.

- *Friendships, new ideas, and defeating resistance become natural.* Living just for today shuts off false motivators, like "Who should I be connecting with? Where should I network? Who's the person making decisions?" You're naturally drawn to others on your same wavelength (thoughts become things), and who would want to do less in their remaining days *when they could do more—skipping, hugging, and laughing?!*

Suddenly, like the air you unthinkingly breathe, friendships, alliances, customers, clients, romantic and business partners become natural extensions of your joy. Practically speaking, planning and connecting for the future, in moderation, are clearly essential, but they ought to be valued as you do them, in the moment, not just for their potential payoff.

- *Challenges begin exciting you.* And then, most interestingly, as you begin radiating in each moment, loving the splendor, you notice opportunities to be who you've never been before, to go where you've never been, and to have what you have never had. You see others taking chances and being rewarded. Seemingly risking all and reaping windfalls. Daring humiliation, yet growing bolder. And you think . . . you wait . . . you wonder "what if," and the next thing you know, you leap, whereupon "lions and tigers and bears" previously unknown to you appear. Yet as you sensed your freedom and remembered your divinity, you will inevitably prevail, dearly grateful that the challenges appeared on your path, because it was them and the path, more than your dreams and the future, that showed you how awesome you really are.

How much can I hedge my bets? Can I agree with what you say and hold on to my old worldviews?

Nothing robs you of your confidence more, nor of your ability to create major life changes, than resting in seemingly safe gray areas of understanding, when within your reach are the black-and-white absolutes of truth. Thinking there are still secrets to your power or that there are universal-forces-unknown that can sway or manipulate the circumstances of your life, you quickly become ineffective. There is only you and your thoughts. Get this, understand *yourself*, and rock your life. Doubt it, and *be* rocked by a world that's seemingly out of your control.

It's not that you must know all things, either about the Universe or about yourself, but that you must know the basics, the simple metaphysical operands, in broad brushstrokes, in order to begin exercising your power. Yet the greatest impediment to doing just this stems from the inherent challenge of living within these jungles, thinking:

1. that you are a mere mortal upon this earth; an afterthought or test subject of an angry god,

2. that life is happening to you instead of understanding that you are "happening" to life, and

3. that to create change, you must react instead of re-envision.

And it's these primitive misunderstandings that create false perceptions from which you begin to feel like a victim, leading to manifestations that only reinforce the original, faulty misunderstandings.

To break this cycle and drill down to the simple, empowering truths that will launch you forward, ask the questions you have to ask, with an open heart and mind, embracing the answers that reveal life's beauty and your power, while leaving no one behind.

What lies beyond life on earth? Beyond reincarnation? Beyond time and space?

For the most part, I don't know. Even I can only see so far based on my perceptions and the limits that make them possible. But, as usual, we can and do know a very, very little bit, which is always enough for peace, clarity, and traction. These are the same little bits anyone can deduce and sense for themselves that speak of either the beauty that will exist or the power they will wield, and that leave no one behind. You and I can deduce that in realms unimaginable, beyond this one:

- we will choose where we go,
- there'll be adventure; we will have fun,
- there'll be learning; we will be challenged,
- we will thrive with an inclination to succeed,
- existence will be based on the pursuit of joy, and
- we will be "in love."

Happy trails, beloved.

EPILOGUE

Now that you've reached the end of this journal, here's what I didn't tell you at the start: these entries have been made over the course of 35 years. Many of them are close to that old. In fact, with the work I've done and the information I've assimilated, I no longer do journal work.

I still have questions, of course, and they still get answered. But whether I'm writing in a Word document, an e-mail, or a business letter, once I start wondering about almost anything, the answers are never far behind. It's like the minds of street-level Mike and higher-self Mike are blending and working together more cohesively, nearly as one. My only complaint, or opportunity (right!), is that it's still not as "automatic" as I'd like, and I usually have to wait around a while for clarity. Small price. Nevertheless, you really should "try this at home"; you must. Might even be easier for you than it's been for me. You'll find a few blank pages at the back of this book to get you started.

Fellow adventurer, you are a pioneer into perhaps the greatest adventure ever conceived of by Divine Mind—life on earth from within the illusions of time and space. Living on the cutting edge of reality creation, of God, by God, for God, yet for now, so far, choosing not to see this. Our civilization, like a teenager in bed on a Sunday morning, now faces the choice to wake up or feign sleep. If we stay in bed, the day will unfold without us, and for every hour delayed, we'll have to play a greater game of catch-up, because while we "sleep" the dog needs walking, our younger siblings need feeding, and some extended family members are going to be showing up early afternoon for the barbeque you promised your parents you'd host while they're out of town. But that's OK! Stress not. You're supernatural, and you do have the ability to bounce back, balance, reconcile, and overachieve like the best of 'em. Besides, your entire slumber, like these words that you're now reading, is merely of a dream within a dream within a dream.

Alternatively, it's still morning. The day's barely begun. You could have a hot shower, brew some fresh coffee, enjoy a little quiet time, and still be among the first in your home to awaken. You might even help to gently wake everyone else, given your jump on the day and your mastery of life's truths. You might whisper in their ears as you walk from room to room that the only things that stand between them and the life of their dreams are the thoughts, words, and action steps they take between now and arrival. Moreover, tell them that where they've been has absolutely no bearing on where they're headed—they get to decide that—which is the real reason they chose to be who they now are, why God chose to be who they now are.

You're getting it. Understand the truth and be free. Understand your spiritual heritage. Understand your inclination to succeed. Understand that you're not being judged. Understand that you're all-powerful with mind-numbing superhero abilities.

Convinced? Do you believe and feel the truth in all that's been written here? Haven't these words spoken of life's beauty, your power, and left no one behind? Is there not logic and heart present? Adventure and fun? Without a single threat? And the freedom to reject what you disagree with and to choose other ideas?

Be happy whatever you choose. You are safe. You are loved. And life on earth is unfolding with flawless grace.

RECOMMENDED
READING

Just as you serendipitously found this book, which was summoned by your own desires "to know" and your showing up in the
world, so have I been drawn to books over the past 30 years that
have especially helped feed my curiosity and improve my life, all
of which are in total alignment with *Life on Earth*:

*The Nature of Personal Reality: Specific, Practical Techniques for
Solving Everyday Problems and Enriching the Life You Know* by
Jane Roberts
    Like all her Seth books (and they're all outstanding), this one
is very deep, objective, and even a bit complex, but I consider Seth
to be the "granddaddy" of all the channeled work in print, both in
content and as a medium for truth conveyance.

*Discover the Power Within You: A Guide to the Unexplored
Depths Within* by Eric Butterworth
    Awesome clarity. Extremely inspirational! Lots of biblical and
Christian references, but explained as I believe they were origi-
nally meant, without the religious spin.

Siddhartha by Hermann Hesse
    Profound wisdom in a timeless, world-famous story.

The Game of Life and How to Play It by Florence Scovel Shinn
Very simple and powerful advice, written in the 1920s. Easy reading for any age.

Life and Teaching of the Masters of the Far East (six-volume set) by Baird T. Spalding
Mind-bending! Volumes 1 and 2 are as adventurous as they are inspirational.

Illusions: The Adventures of a Reluctant Messiah and *Jonathan Livingston Seagull* by Richard Bach
Exhilarating, fun, and easy to read. These two novels are on almost everyone's list—for good reason!

Journeys Out of the Body by Robert Monroe
The classic on out-of-body experiences.

Life After Life: The Investigation of a Phenomenon—Survival of Bodily Death by Raymond A. Moody, Jr., M.D., and a foreword by Elisabeth Kübler-Ross, M.D.
The classic on life after life and near-death experiences.

Conversations with God: An Uncommon Dialogue by Neale Donald Walsch
Each of the books in this series is a mind-blower. They're also very easy and fun to read.

Emmanuel's Book: A Manual for Living Comfortably in the Cosmos by Pat Rodegast and Judith Stanton
The entire series of Emmanuel books offers gentle yet powerful reminders of how angelic we all are. Wonderful.

Ramtha: The White Book by Ramtha
Very friendly, powerful, and inspirational. Another easy read and one of the most powerful of all the titles listed here.

The Prophet by Kahlil Gibran

Insight into life's most basic truths. Another perennial, international bestseller.

You Can Heal Your Life by Louise Hay

Very clearly written by a fellow "life adventurer" who deeply understands that *we cause that which hurts us*, and we can therefore heal it too. The second half of this book contains the most impressive index of common physical ailments and their likely causes that I have ever read.

The Science of Getting Rich by Wallace D. Wattles

If you've ever thought that you might like wealth, you'll love this. A truly unique and encouraging perspective.

Messages from Michael by Chelsea Quinn Yarbro

Very "out there," yet ringing of truth and containing revolutionary material I've not thought of or heard of elsewhere. Helps me to be less critical of others and more patient with myself.

Atlas Shrugged and *The Fountainhead* by Ayn Rand

Although Ayn Rand was an atheist, I believe her books are extremely spiritual in that she considered herself a "man worshiper" and she reveled in the glory of life and our ability to master life's elements. Her epic novels are spellbinding, romantic, and deeply philosophical, and her talent is off the charts.

The Secret (DVD and book) by Rhonda Byrne

I'm grateful to have been one of the featured teachers in this outstanding documentary on the law of attraction. It's as inspirational as it is enlightening.

ABOUT THE
AUTHOR

Mike Dooley is a former PricewaterhouseCoopers international tax consultant turned entrepreneur. He's the founder of a philosophical Adventurers Club on the Internet that's now home to more than 725,000 members from 182 countries. His inspirational books emphasizing spiritual accountability have been published in 25 languages, and he was one of the featured teachers in the international phenomenon *The Secret*. Today Mike is best known for his free "Notes from the Universe" e-mailings, social network postings, and his *New York Times* bestsellers *Infinite Possibilities: The Art of Living Your Dreams* and *Leveraging the Universe: 7 Steps to Engaging Life's Magic*. Mike lives what he teaches, traveling internationally to speak on life, dreams, and happiness.

For more information on Mike's work, or to receive his free daily *Notes from the Universe* e-mailings, please visit www.tut.com.

Questions & Answers from My Higher Self

Questions & Answers from My Higher Self

Questions & Answers from My Higher Self

Questions & Answers from My Higher Self

_____
_____
_____
_____
_____
_____
_____
_____
_____
_____
_____
_____
_____
_____
_____
_____
_____
_____
_____
_____
_____
_____
_____

HAY HOUSE TITLES OF RELATED INTEREST

YOU CAN HEAL YOUR LIFE, the movie,
starring Louise Hay & Friends
(available as a 1-DVD program and an expanded 2-DVD set)
Watch the trailer at: www.LouiseHayMovie.com

THE SHIFT, the movie,
starring Dr. Wayne W. Dyer
(available as a 1-DVD program and an expanded 2-DVD set)
Watch the trailer at: www.DyerMovie.com

E-CUBED:
*Nine More Energy Experiments That Prove Manifesting Magic
and Miracles Is Your Full-Time Gig,* by Pam Grout

THE GAME OF LIFE AND HOW TO PLAY IT,
by Florence Scovel Shinn

ENOUGH ALREADY:
The Power of Radical Contentment, by Alan Cohen

NOTHING CHANGES UNTIL YOU DO:
A Guide to Self-Compassion and Getting Out of Your Own Way,
by Mike Robbins

RESILIENCE FROM THE HEART:
The Power to Thrive in Life's Extremes, by Gregg Braden

All of the above are available at your local bookstore,
or may be ordered by contacting Hay House (see next page).